Confessions of a Book-Lover

Maurice Francis Egan

Alpha Editions

This edition published in 2021

ISBN : 9789355899699

Design and Setting By
Alpha Editions
www.alphaedis.com
Email – info@alphaedis.com

As per information held with us this book is in Public Domain. This book is a reproduction of an important historical work. Alpha Editions uses the best technology to reproduce historical work in the same manner it was first published to preserve its original nature. Any marks or number seen are left intentionally to preserve its true form.

CHAPTER I

My Boyhood Reading

Early Recollections

To get the best out of books, I am convinced that you must begin to love these perennial friends very early in life. It is the only way to know all their "curves," all those little shadows of expression and small lights. There is a glamour which you never *see* if you begin to read with a serious intention late in life, when questions of technique and grammar and mere words begin to seem too important.

Then you have become too critical to feel through all Fenimore Cooper's verbiage the real lakes and woods, or the wild fervour of romance beneath dear Sir Walter's mat of words. You lose the unreclaimable flavour of books. A friend you may irretrievably lose when you lose a friend—if you are so deadly unfortunate as to lose a friend—for even the memories of him are embittered; but no great author can ever have done anything that will make the book you love less precious to you.

The new school of pedagogical thought disapproves, I know, of miscellaneous reading, and no modern moralist will agree with Madame de Sévigné that "bad books are better than no books at all"; but Madame de Sévigné may have meant books written in a bad style, or feeble books, and not books bad in the moral sense. However, I must confess that when I was young, I read several books which I was told afterward were very bad indeed. But I did not find this out until somebody told me! The youthful mind must possess something of the quality attributed to a duck's back! I recall that once "The Confessions of Rousseau" was snatched suddenly away from me by a careful mother just as I had begun to think that Jean Jacques was a very interesting man and almost as queer as some of the people I knew. I believe that if I had been allowed to finish the book, it would have become by some mental chemical process a very edifying criticism of life.

"Tom Jones" I found in an attic and I was allowed to read it by a pious aunt, whom I was visiting, because she mixed it up with "Tom Brown of Rugby"; but I found it even more tiresome than "Eric, or Little by Little," for which I dropped it. I remember, too, that I was rather shocked by some things written in the Old Testament; and I retorted to my aunt's pronouncement that she considered "the 'Arabian Nights' a dangerous book," by saying that the Old Testament was the worst book I had ever read; but I supposed "people had put something into it when God wasn't looking." She sent me home.

At home, I was permitted to read only the New Testament. On winter Sunday afternoons, when there was nothing else to do, I became sincerely attached to the Acts of the Apostles. And I came to the conclusion that nobody could tell a short story as well as Our Lord Himself. The Centurion was one of my favourite characters. He seemed to be such a good soldier; and his plea, "Lord, I am not worthy," flashes across my mental vision every day of my life.

In the Catholic churches, a part of the Gospel is read every Sunday, and carefully interpreted. This always interested me because I knew in advance what the priest was going to read. Most of the children of my acquaintance were taught their Scriptures through the International Sunday-school lessons, and seemed to me to be submerged in the geography of Palestine and other tiresome details. For me, reading as I did, the whole of the New Testament was radiant with interest, a frankly human interest. There were many passages that I did not pretend to understand, sometimes because the English was obscure or archaic, and sometimes because my mind was not equal to it or my knowledge too small. Whatever may be the opinion of other people, mine is that the reading of the New Testament in the simplicity of childhood, with the flower of intuition not yet blighted, is one of the most beautiful of mental experiences. In my own case, it gave a glow to life; it caused me to distinguish between truth and fairy tales, between fact and fiction—and this is often very difficult for an imaginative child.

This kind of reading implies leisure and the absence of distraction. Unhappily, much leisure does not seem to be left for the modern child. The unhappy creature is even told that there will be "something in Heaven for children to do!" As to distractions, the modern child is surrounded by them; and it appears to be one of the main intentions of the present system of instruction not to leave to a child any moments of leisure for the indulgence of the imagination. But I am not offering the example of my childhood for imitation by the modern parents.

Nevertheless, it had great consolations. There were no "movies" in those days, and the theatre was only occasionally permitted; but on long afternoons, after you had learned to read, you might lose yourself in "The Scottish Chiefs" to your heart's content. It seems to me that the beauty of this fashion of leisurely reading was that you had time to visualize everything, and you felt the dramatic moments so keenly, that a sense of unreality never obtruded itself at the wrong time. It was not necessary for you to be told that Helen Mar was beautiful. It was only necessary for her to say, in tones so entrancing that you heard them, "My Wallace!" to know that she was the loveliest person in all Scotland. But "The Scottish Chiefs" required the leisure of long holiday afternoons, especially as the copy I read had been so misused that I had to spend precious half hours in putting the pages together. It was worth the trouble, however.

Before I could read, I was compelled on rainy days to sit at my mother's knee and listen to what *she* read. I am happy to say that she never read children's books. Nothing was ever adapted to my youthful misunderstanding. She read aloud what she liked to read, and she never considered whether I liked it or not. It was a method of discipline. At first, I looked drearily out at the soggy city street, in which rivulets of melted snow made any exercise, suitable to my age, impossible. There is nothing so hopeless for a child as an afternoon in a city when the heavy snows begin to melt. My mother, however, was altogether regardless of what happened outside of the house. At two o'clock precisely—after the manner of the King in William Morris's "Earthly Paradise"—she waved her wand. After that, all that I was expected to do was to make no noise.

In this way I became acquainted with "The Virginians," then running in *Harper's Magazine*, with "Adam Bede" and "As You Like It" and "Richard III." and "Oliver Twist" and "Nicholas Nickleby" and "Valentine Vox"— why "Valentine Vox?"—and other volumes when I should have been listening to "Alice in Wonderland." But when I came, in turn, to "Alice in Wonderland," I found Alice's rather dull in comparison with the adventures of the Warrington brothers. And Thackeray's picture of Gumbo carrying in the soup tureen! To have listened to Rebecca's description of the great fight in "Ivanhoe," to have lived through the tournament of Ashby de la Zouche, was a poor preparation for the vagaries of the queer creatures that surrounded the inimitable Alice.

There appeared to be no children's books in the library to which we had access. It never seemed to me that "Robinson Crusoe" or "Gulliver's Travels" or "Swiss Family Robinson" were children's books; they were not so treated by my mother, and I remember, as a small boy, going up to Chestnut Street in Philadelphia, with divine eagerness, to buy the latest number of a Dickens serial. I think the name of the shop—the shop of Paradise—which sold these books was called Ashburnham's. It may be asked how the episode in "Adam Bede" of Hetty and that of "little Em'ly" in Dickens struck the child mind. As I remember, the child mind was awed and impressed, by a sense of horror, probably occasioned as much by the force of the style, by the suggestions of an unknown terror, as by any facts which a child could grasp.

It was a curious thing that my mother, who had remarkably good taste in literature, admired Mrs. Henry Wood extravagantly. She also admired Queen Victoria. She never read "East Lynne" aloud, because, I gathered, she considered it "improper"; and Miss Braddon's "Lady Audley's Secret" came under the same ban, though I heard it talked of frequently. It was difficult to discover where my mother drew the line between what was "proper" and what was "not proper." Shakespeare she seemed to regard as eminently proper, and, I noticed, hesitated and mumbled only when she came to certain parts of Ophelia's song. It seems strange now that I never rated Mrs. Henry Wood's novels with those of George Eliot or Thackeray or Dickens. There seemed to be some imperceptible difference which my mother never explained, but which I, instinctively, understood; and when Anthony Trollope's "Orley Farm" was read, I placed him above Mrs. Henry Wood, but not on an equality with Dickens or Thackeray.

Harper's Magazine, in those days, contained great treasure! There, for instance, were the delightful articles by Porte Crayon—General Strothers, I think. These one listened to with pleasure; but the bane of my existence was Mr. Abbott's "Life of Napoleon Bonaparte." It seemed to me as if it would never end, and it stretched as dolorously before me as that other fearful process which appalled my waking days—the knowledge that all my life I should be obliged to clean my teeth three times a day with powdered charcoal!

After a time, I began to read for myself; but the delights of desultory reading were gloomed by the necessity of studying long lessons that no emancipated child of to-day would endure. Misguided people sometimes came to the school and told childish stories, at which we all laughed, but which even the most illiterate despised. To have known George Warrington, to have mingled familiarly in the society of George Washington, to remember the picture of Beatrix Esmond coming down the stairs—I am not speaking of Du Maurier's travesties of that delightful book—to have seen the old ladies in "Cranford," sucking their oranges in the privacies of their rooms, made one despise foolish little tales about over-industrious bees and robins which seemed not even to have the ordinary common sense of geese!

Suddenly, my mother became a devout Catholic. The scene changed. On one unhappy Sunday afternoon "Monte Cristo" was rudely snatched from my entranced hands. Dumas was on the list of the "improper," and to this day I have never finished the episodes in which I was so deeply interested. Now the wagon of the circulating library ceased to come as in the old days. The children of the neighbours offered me Sunday-school books, taken from the precious store of the Methodist Sunday School opposite our house. They seemed to me to be stupid beyond all words. There was not one really good fight in them all, and after an honest villain like Brian de Bois Guilbert, the bad people in these volumes were very lacking in stamina. The "Rollo" books were gay compared to them. I concluded that if anything on earth could make a child hate religion, it was the perusal of these unreal books. My mother saw that I had Alban Butler's "Lives of the Saints" for Sunday reading. They were equally dull; and other "Lives," highly recommended, were quite as uninspiring as the little volumes from the Protestant library. They were generally translated from the French, without vitality and without any regard for the English idiom. I recall, through the mists, sitting down one Sunday afternoon, to read "The Life of Saint Rose of Lima." As it concerned itself with South America, it seemed to me that there might be in it a good fighter or two; or, at least, somebody might cut off the ear of a High Priest's servant as was done in the New Testament. But no, I was shocked to read in the very beginning, that

so pure was the little Saint, even in her infancy, that when her uncle, who was her godfather, kissed her after her baptism, a rosy glow, a real blush of shame, overspread her countenance.

In that book I read no more that day!

But I discovered a volume I have never forgotten, which probably after "The Young Marooners," had the greatest influence on me for a short period. This was "Fabiola," by Cardinal Wiseman. There was good stuff in it; it made me feel proud to be a Christian; it was full of thrills; and it taught a lot about the archæology of Rome, for it was part of that excellent story. I have always looked on "Fabiola" as a very great book. Then at Christmas, when my father gave me "The Last Days of Pompeii," I was in a new world, not alien to the world of "Fabiola," but in some way supplementary to it. This gift was accompanied by Washington Irving's "Tales of the Alhambra." *Conspuez les livres des poupées!* What nice little story books, arranged for the growing mind, could awaken such visions of the past, such splendid arabesques and trailing clouds of glory as this book! Read at the right time, it makes the pomegranate and the glittering crescents live forever, and creates a love for Spain and a romance of old Spain which can never die.

After this, I had a cold mental douche. I was given "Les Enfants des Bois," by Elie Berthet in French, to translate word for word. It was a horrible task, and the difficulties of the verbs and the laborious research in the dictionary prevented me from enjoying the adventures of these infants. I cannot remember anything that happened to them; but I know that the book gave me an ever-enduring distrust of the subjunctive mood in the Gallic language. Somebody had left about a copy of a French romance called "Les Aventures de Polydore Marasquin." It was of things that happened to a man in a kingdom of monkeys. It went very well, with an occasional use of the dictionary, until I discovered that the gentleman was about to engage himself to a very attractive monkeyess. I gave up the book in disgust, but I have since discovered that there have been lately several imitators of these adventures, which I think were written by an author named Léon Gozlan.

About this time, the book auction became a fashion in Philadelphia. If your people had respect for art, they invariably subscribed to a publication called the *Cosmopolitan Art Magazine*, and you received a steel engraving of

Shakespeare and his Friends, with Sir Walter Raleigh very much in the foreground, wearing a beautifully puffed doublet and very well-fitting hose, and another steel engraving of Washington at Lexington. If your people were interested in literature, they frequented the book auctions. My father had a great respect for what he called "classical literature." He considered Cowper's "The Task" immensely classical; it was beautifully bound, and he never read it. One day he secured a lovely edition of the "Complete Works of Thomas Moore." It had been a subject of much competition at the auction, and was cherished accordingly. The binding was tooled. It was put on the centre table and adored as a work of art. Here was richness!

Tom Moore's long poems are no doubt classed at present as belonging to those old and faded gardens in which "The Daisy" and "The Keepsake," by Lady Blessington, once flourished; but if I could only recall the pleasure I had in the reading of "Lalla Rookh" and "The Veiled Prophet of Korhasson," I think I should be very happy. And the notes to "Lalla Rookh" and to Moore's prose novel of "The Epicurean"! "The Epicurean" was not much of a novel, but the notes were full of amazing Egyptian mysteries, which seemed quite as splendid as the machinery in the "Arabian Nights." The notes to "Lalla Rookh" smelled of roses, and I remember as a labour of love copying out all the allusions to roses in these notes with the intention of writing about them when I grew up. My mother objected to the translations from Anacreon; she said they were "improper"; but my father said that he had been assured on competent authority that they were "classic," and of course that settled it. There was no story in them, and they seemed to me to be stupid.

Just about this time, one of the book auctions yielded up a copy of the "Complete Works of Miss Mitford." You perhaps can imagine how a city boy, who was allowed to spend two weeks each year at the most on the arid New Jersey seacoast, fell upon "Our Village." It became an incentive for long walks, in the hope of finding some country lanes and something resembling the English primroses. I read and reread "Our Village" until I could close my eyes at any time and see the little world in which Miss Mitford lived. I tried to read her tragedy, "The Two Foscari." A tragedy had a faint interest; but, being exiled to the attic for some offense against the conventionalities demanded of a Philadelphia child, with no book but Miss Mitford's, I spent my time looking up all the references to roses in her tragedies. These I combined with the knowledge acquired from Tom Moore, and made notes for a paper to be printed in some great periodical in the future. Why roses? Why Miss Mitford and roses? Why Tom Moore and roses? I do not know, but, when I was sixteen years of age, I printed the paper in *Appleton's Journal*, where it may still be found. My parents, who did not look on my literary attempts, at the expense of mathematics, with favour, suggested that I was a plagiarist, but as I had no time to look up the meaning of the word in the dictionary, I let it go. It simply struck me as one of those evidences of misunderstanding which every honest artist must be content to accept.

My mother, evidently fearing the influence of "classical" literature, gave me one day "The Parent's Assistant," by Miss Edgeworth. I think that it was in this book that I discovered "Rosamond; or The Purple Jar" and the story of the good boy or girl who never cut the bit of string that tied a package; I sedulously devoted myself to the imitation of this economic child, and was very highly praised for getting the best out of a good book until I broke a tooth in trying to undo a very tough knot.

It was a far cry from the respectable Miss Edgeworth to a series of Beadle's "Dime Novels." I looked on them as delectable but inferior. There was a prejudice against them in well-brought-up households; but if you thoughtfully provided yourself with a brown paper cover, which concealed the flaring yellow of Beadle's front page, you were very likely to escape criticism. I never finished "Osceola, the Seminole," because my aunt looked over my shoulder and read a rapturous account of a real fight, in which somebody kicked somebody else violently in the abdomen. My aunt reported to my mother that the book was very "indelicate" and after that Beadle's "Dime Novels" were absolutely forbidden. At school, we were told that any boy who read Beadle's was a moral leper; but as most of us concluded that leper had something to do with leaper, the effect was not very convincing.

Perhaps I might have been decoyed back to Beadle's, for all the youngsters knew that there was nothing really wrong in them, but I happened to remember the scene in Sir Walter Scott's "Abbot," where Edward Glendenning wades into the sea to prevent Mary Stuart from leaving Scotland. I hied me to "The Monastery" and devoured everything of Sir Walter's except "Saint Ronan's Well." That never seemed worthy of the great Sir Walter. "The Black Dwarf" and "Anne of Geierstein" were rather tough reading, and "Count Robert of Paris" might have been written by Lord Bacon, if Lord Bacon had been a contemporary of Sir Walter's. "Peveril of the Peak" and "Ivanhoe" and "Bride of Lammermoor" again and again dazzled and consoled me until I discovered "Nicholas Nickleby."

"Nicholas Nickleby" took entire possession of me. In the rainy winter afternoons, when nothing could occur out of doors which a respectable city boy was permitted to indulge in, I found that I was expected to work. Boys worked hard at their lessons in those days. There was a kitchen downstairs with a Dutch oven not used in the winter. There it was easy to build a small fire and to toast bread and to read "Nicholas Nickleby" after one had rushed through the required tasks, which generally included ten pages of the "Historia Sacra" in Latin. If you never read "Nicholas Nickleby" when you were young, you cannot possibly know the flavour of Dickens. You can't laugh now as you laughed then. Oh, the delight of Mr. Crummles's description of his wife's dignified manner of standing with her head on a spear!

The tragedy in "Nicholas Nickleby" never appealed to me. It was necessary to skip that. When the people were gentlemanly and ladylike, they became great bores. But what young reader of Dickens can forget the hostile attitude of Mr. Lillyvick, great-uncle of the little Miss Kenwigses, when Nicholas attempted to teach them French? As one grows older, even Mr. Squeers and 'Tilda give one less real delight; but think of the first discovery of them, and it is like Balboa's—or was it Cortez's?—discovery of the Pacific in Keats's sonnet. "Nicholas Nickleby" was read over and over again, with unfailing pleasure. I found "Little Dorrit" rather tiresome; "Barnaby Rudge" and "A Tale of Two Cities" seemed to be rather serious reading, not quite Dickensish enough for my taste, yet better than anything else that anybody had written. My later impressions of Dickens modified these instinctive intuitions.

One day, a set of Thackeray arrived, little green volumes, as I remember, and I began to read "Vanity Fair." My mother seized it and read it aloud again. Her confessor had told her that a dislike for good novels was "Puritan" and she, shocked by the implied reproach, took again to novel reading. I am afraid that I disliked Colonel Dobbin and Amelia very much. Becky Sharp pleased me beyond words; I don't think that the morality of the case affected my point of view at all. I was delighted whenever Becky "downed" an enemy. They were such a lot of stupid people—the enemies—and I reflected during the course of the story that, after all, Thackeray had said that poor Becky had no mother to guide her footsteps. When the Marquis of Steyne was hit on the forehead with the diamonds, I thought it served him right; but I was unhappy because poor Becky had lost the jewels. In finishing the book with those lovely Thackerayan cadences, my mother said severely, "That is what always happens to bad people!" But in my heart I did not believe that Becky Sharp was a bad person at all.

For a time I returned to Dickens, to "Nicholas Nickleby," to "David Copperfield." I respected Thackeray. He had gripped me in some way that I could not explain. But Dickens I loved. Later—it was on one June afternoon I think—when the news of Dickens's death arrived, it seemed to me that for a while all delight in life had ended.

One of those experts in psychology who are always seeking questions sometime ago wrote to me demanding if "Plutarch's Lives" had influenced me, and whether I thought they were good reading for the young. Our "Plutarch" was rather appalling to look at. It was bound in mottled cardboard, and the pages had red edges; but I attacked it one day, when I was about ten years of age, and became enthralled. It was "actual." My mother was a veteran politician, and read a daily paper, with Southern tendencies called the *Age*; my father belonged to the opposite party, and admired Senator Hoar as greatly as my mother admired the famous Vallandigham. Between the two, I had formed a very poor opinion of American statesmen in general; but the statesmen in "Plutarch" were of a very different type.

Julius Cæsar interested me; but Brutus filled me with exaltation. I had not then read Shakespeare's "Julius Cæsar." It seemed to me that Brutus was a model for all time. Now, understand I was a good Christian child, and I said my prayers every night and morning, but this did not prevent me from hating the big bully of the school, who made the lives of the ten or fifteen small boys a perpetual torment. How we suffered, no adult human tongue can tell—and our tongues never told because it was a convention that tales should not be told out of school. One of the pleasant tricks of the bully and his friends was to chase the little boys after school in the winter and bury them until they were almost suffocated in the snow which was piled up in the narrow streets. It was not only suffocating snow, but it was dirty snow. It happened that I had been presented with a penknife consisting of two rather leaden blades covered with a brilliant iridescent mother-of-pearl handle. The bully wanted this knife, and I knew it. Generally, I left it at home; but it occurred to me on one inspired morning, after I had read "Plutarch" the night before, that I would display the knife open in my pocket, and when he threw the full weight of his body upon me, I would kill him at once, by an upward thrust of the knife.

This struck me as a good deed entirely worthy of Brutus. Of course, I knew that I should be hanged, but then I expected the glory of making a last dying speech, and, besides, the school would have a holiday. On the morning preceding the great sacrifice, I gave out dark hints to the small boys, distributed my various belongings to friends who were about to be bereaved, and predicted a coming holiday. I was looked on as rather "crazy," but I reflected that I would soon be considered heroic, and my friends gladly accepted the gifts.

The fatal afternoon came. I displayed the penknife. The chase began. The bully and his chosen friends threw themselves upon me. The moment had come; I thrust the knife upward; the big boy uttered a howl, and ran, still howling. I looked for blood, but there was none visible; I came to the conclusion, with satisfaction, that he was bleeding internally. I spent a gloomy evening at home uttering dire predictions which were incomprehensible to the members of my family, and reread Brutus, in the "Lives."

The next morning I went to school with lessons unstudied and awaited events. The mother of the bully appeared, and entered into an excited colloquy with the very placid and dignified teacher. I announced to the boy next to me, "My time has come." I was called up to the awful desk. "Is he dead?" I asked. "Did he bleed internally?" "You little wretch," the mother of the tyrant said, "you cut such fearful holes in my son's coat, that he is afraid to come to school to-day!" Then I said, regretfully, "Oh, I hoped that I had killed him." There was a sensation; my character was blackened. I was set down as a victim of total depravity; I endured it all, but I knew in my heart that it was "Plutarch." This is the effect that "Plutarch" had on the mind of a good Christian child.

The effects of "Plutarch" on my character were never discovered at home, and as I grew older and learned one or two wrestling tricks, the bully let me alone. Besides, my murderous intention, which had leaked out, gave me such a reputation that I became a dictator myself, and made terms for the small boys, in the name of freedom, which were sometimes rather despotic.

It was also during these days that I remember carrying confusion into the family when a patronizing, intellectual lady called and said, "I hope that this dear little boy is reading the Rollo books?" "No," I answered quickly and indiscreetly, "I am reading 'The New Magdalen,' by Wilkie Collins." I did not think much of Wilkie Collins until I read "The Moonstone." It seemed that "The New Magdalen" had been purchased inadvertently by my father, in a packet of "classics."

My father generally arrived at home late in the afternoon, when he read the evening paper. After a very high tea, he stretched himself on a long horsehair-covered sofa, and bade me read to him, generally from the novels of George Eliot, or from certain romances running through the New York *Ledger* by Sylvanus Cobb, Jr. These were generally stories of the times of the Irish Kings, in which gallowglasses and lovely and aristocratic Celtic maidens disported themselves. My mother, after her conversion, disapproved of the New York *Ledger*. In fact, there were families in Philadelphia whose heads regarded it with real horror! In our house, there was a large stack of this interesting periodical, which, with many volumes of Godey's *Lady's Book*, were packed in the attic.

It happened that a young man, in whom my father had a great interest, was threatened with tuberculosis. An awful rumour was set abroad that he was about to die. He sent over a messenger asking my father for the back numbers of the New York *Ledger* containing a long serial story by Mrs. Anna Cora Mowatt. As I remember, it was a story of the French Revolution, and the last number that I was allowed to read ended with a description of a dance in an old château, when the Marquise, who was floating through the minuet, suddenly discovered blood on the white-kid glove of her right hand! I was never permitted to discover where the blood came from; I should like to find out now if I could find the novel. I remember that my mother was terribly shocked when my father sent the numbers of the New York *Ledger* to the apparently dying man. "It's a horrible thing," my mother said, "to think of any Christian person reading the New York *Ledger* at the point of death." The young man, however, did not die; and I rather think my father attributed his recovery to the exhilarating effect of one of his favourite stories.

There were certain other serial stories I was ordered to read; they were stories of the Irish Brigade in France. My mother, I remember, disapproved of them because Madame de Pompadour was frequently mentioned, and she thought that my father regarded the lady in question too tolerantly. These romances were, I think, written by a certain Myles O'Reilly who was in some way connected with the army. This procedure of reading aloud was not always agreeable, as my father frequently went to sleep in the middle of a passage and forgot what I had already read. The consequence was that I was obliged to begin the same old story over again on the following evening.

It happened that my father was one of the directors of a local library, and in it I found Bates's volume on the Amazon—I forget the exact title of the book. I found myself in a new world; I lived in Para; I tried to manufacture an imitation of the Urari poison with a view to exterminating rats in the warehouse by the use of arrows; I lived and had my being in the forests of Brazil; and I produced, at intervals, a thrilling novel, with the glowing atmosphere of the Amazon as a background. I preferred Mr. Bates to any novelist I had ever read. He held possession of my imagination, until he was forced out by a Mr. Jerningham who wrote a most entrancing book on Brittany. Saint Malo became the only town for me; I adored Henri de la Rochejaquelein; and the Stuarts, whom I had learned to love at the knees of Sir Walter Scott, were displaced by the Vendéans.

Noticing that I was devoted to books of travel, my father asked me to parse Kane's "Arctic Voyages." I found the volumes cold and repellent. They gave me a rooted prejudice against the North Pole which even the adventure of Doctor Cook has never enabled me to overcome.

About this time, my mother began to feel that I needed to read something more gentle, which would root me more effectively in my religion. She began, I think, with Cardinal Newman's "Callista" in which there was a thrilling chapter called "The Possession of Juba." It seemed to me one of the most stirring things I had ever read. Then I was presented with Mrs. Sadlier's "The Blakes and the Flanagans," which struck me as a very delightful satire, and with a really interesting novel of New York called "Rosemary," by Dr. J. V. Huntington; and then a terribly blood-curdling story of the Carbonari in

Italy, called "Lionello." After this I was wafted into a series of novels by Julia Kavanagh; "Natalie," and "Bessie," and "Seven Years," I think were the principals. My father declined to read them; he thought they were too sentimental, but as the author had an Irish name he was inclined to regard them with tolerance. He thought I would be better employed in absorbing "Tom and Jerry; or The Adventures of Corinthian Bob," by Pierce Egan. My mother objected to this, and substituted "Lady Violet; or the Wonder of Kingswood Chace," by the younger Pierce Egan, which she considered more moral.

My father was very generous at Christmas, and I bought a large volume of Froissart for two dollars and a half at an old book stand on Fifth Street, near Spruce. After this, I was lost to the world during the Christmas holidays. After breakfast, I saturated myself with the delightful battles in that precious book.

My principal duty was to look after the front pavement. In the spring and summer, it was carefully washed twice a week and reddened with some kind of paint, which always accompanied a box of fine white sand for the scouring of the marble steps; but in the winter, this respectable sidewalk had to be kept free from snow and ice.

Hitherto my battle with the elements had been rather a diversion. Besides, I was in competition with the other small boys in the block—or in the "square," as we Philadelphians called it. Now it became irksome; I neglected to dig the ice from between the bricks; I skimped my cleaning of the gutter; I forgot to put on my "gums." The boy next door became a mirror of virtue; he was quoted to me as one whose pavement was a model to all the neighbours; indeed, it was rumoured that the Mayor passing down our street, had stopped and admired the working of his civic spirit, while the result of my efforts was passed by with evident contempt. I did not care. I hugged Froissart to my heart. Who would condescend to wield a broom and a wooden shovel, even for the reward of ten cents in cash, when he could throw javelins and break lances with the knights of the divine Froissart? The end of my freedom came after this. The terrible incident of the Mayor's contempt, invented, I believe, by the boy next door, induced my mother to believe that I was not only losing my morals, but becoming too much of a book-worm. For many long weeks I was deprived of any amusing book except "Robinson Crusoe." After this interval, vacation came; I seemed to have grown older, and books were never quite the same again.

In the vacation, however, when the days were very long and there was a great deal of leisure, I found myself reduced to Grimms' "Fairy Tales" and a delightful volume by Madame Perrault, and I was even then very much struck by the difference. Of course I read Grimm from cover to cover, and went back again over the pages, hoping that I had neglected something. The homeliness of the stories touched me; it seemed to me that you found yourself in the atmosphere of old Germany. Madame Perrault was more delicate; her fairy tales were pictures of no life that ever existed, and there was a great dissimilarity between her "Cendrillon" and the Grimms' story of "Aschenputtel." As I remember, the haughty sisters in the story of the beautiful girl who lived among the ashes each cut off one of her toes, in order to make her feet seem smaller and left bloody marks on the glass slipper. Madame Perrault's slipper was, I think, of white fur, and there was no such brutality in *her* fairyland. But, except Hans Christian Andersen's, there are no such gripping fairy tales as those of the Brethren Grimm. During this vacation, too, I discovered the "Leprachaun," the little Irish fairy with the hammer. He was not at all like the English fairies in Shakespeare's "Midsummer Night's Dream," and, leaving out Ariel, I think I liked him best of all.

That summer, too, I found an old copy of "Midsummer Night's Dream" in the attic. The print was exceedingly fine, but everything was there. No doubt there is much to be said by the pedagogues in favour of scrupulously studying Shakespeare's plays; but if you have never discovered "As You Like It" or "Midsummer Night's Dream" when you were very young, you will never know the meaning of that light which never was on land or sea, and with which Keats surrounds us in the "Ode to the Nightingale." The love interest did not count much. In my youthful experience everybody either married or died, in books. That was to be expected. It was the atmosphere that counted. One could see the troopers coming into the open space in the Forest of Arden and hear their songs, making the leaves of the trees quiver before they appeared. And Puck! and Caliban! When I was young I was always very sorry for Caliban, and, being very religious, I felt that the potent Prospero might have done something for his soul.

There was a boy who lived near us called Lawrence Stockdale—peace be to his ashes where-ever he rests! His father and mother, who were persons of cultivation, encouraged him to read, but we were not of one opinion on any subject. He was devoted to Dumas, the Elder. After the episode of "Monte Cristo" I was led to believe that Dumas was "wrong." I preferred Sir Walter Scott, and loved all the Stuarts, having a positive devotion for Mary, Queen of Scots. One day, however, I discovered somewhere, under a pile of old geometries and books about navigation, a fat, red-bound copy of "Boccaccio." Stockdale said that "Boccaccio" was "wronger" than Dumas, and that his people had warned him against the stories of this Italian. As we lived near an Italian colony, and he disliked Italians, while I loved them, I attributed this to mere prejudice.

The "Boccaccio" was, as I have said, fat and large. For a boy who likes to read, a fat book is very tempting, and just as I had seated myself one afternoon on the front doorstep, to read the story of the Falcon, and having finished it with great pleasure, dipped into another tale not so edifying, my mother appeared. She turned pale with horror, and seized the book at once. My father was informed of what had occurred. He was little alarmed, I think. My mother said: "We shall have to change the whole course of this boy's reading." "We shall have to change the boy first," my father said, with a sigh. But this was not the end. At the proper time I was led to the Pastor, who was my mother's confessor. The book was presented to him for destruction.

"It's a bad book," the Monsignore said. "I hope you didn't talk about any of these stories to the other boys in school?"

"Oh, no," I said; "if I did, they would say much worse things, and I would probably have to tell them in confession. Besides," I added, "all the people in the Boccaccio book were good Catholics, I suppose, as they were Italians, and I think, after all, when they caught the plague, they died good deaths."

The Pastor looked puzzled, took the book, and gave me his blessing and dismissed me. And my mother seemed to think that I was sufficiently exorcised.

After this the books I read were more carefully considered. I was given the "Tales of Canon Schmidt"—dear little stories of German children in the Black Forest, with strange little wood-cuts, which went very well with another volume I found at this time called "Jack Halifax," not "John Halifax, Gentleman," which my mother had already read to me—but a curious little tome long out of print. And then there sailed upon my vision a long procession of the works of the Flemish novelist, Hendrik Conscience, whose "Lion of Flanders" opened a new world of romance, and there were "Wooden Clara," and other pieces which made one feel as if one lived in Flanders.

Just about this time I read in Littell's *Living Age* a novel called "The Amber Witch," and some of Fritz Reuter's Low German stories; but these were all effaced by "The Quaker Soldier." This may not have been much of a novel. I did not put it to the touch of comparison with "The Virginians" or "Esmond." They were what my father called "classics"—things superior and apart; but "The Quaker Soldier" was quite good enough for me. It opened a new view of American Revolutionary history, and then it was redolent of the country of Pennsylvania. I recall now the incident of the Pennsylvania Dutch housewife's using her thumb to spread the butter on the bread for the hungry soldier. This is all that I can recall of those delectable pages. But, later, neither Henry Peterson's "Pemberton" nor Dr. Weir Mitchell's "Hugh Wynne" seemed to have the glory and the fascination of the long-lost "Quaker Soldier."

After this, I fell under the spell of the French Revolution through a book, given to me by my mother, about *la Vendée*. It was a dull book, but nothing, not even a bad translation, could dim the heroism of Henri de la Rochejaquelein for me, and I became a Royalist of the Royalists, and held hotly the thesis that if George Washington had returned the compliment of going over to France in '89, he would have done Lafayette a great service by restoring the good Louis XVI. and the beautiful Marie Antoinette!

When I had reached the age of seventeen I had developed, as the result of my reading, a great belief in all lost causes. I had become exceedingly devoted to the cause of Ireland as the kindly Pastor had sent me a copy of "Willy Reilly and His Colleen Bawn," perhaps as an antidote to the lingering effects of "Boccaccio." I was rather troubled to find so many "swear words" in it, but I made all the allowances that a real lover of literature is often compelled to make!

The Bible

The glimpses I had of the Bible, some of which rather prejudiced me, as a moral child, against the Sacred Book, were, however, of inestimable value. Of course the New Testament was always open to me, and I read it constantly as a pleasure. The language, both in the Douai version and the King James version, was often very obscure. Although I soon learned to recognize the beauty of the 23rd Psalm in the King James version—which I always read when I went to one of my cousins—I found the sonorous Latinisms of the Douai version interesting. For a time I was limited to a book of Bible stories given us to read at school, as it was considered unwise to permit children to read the Old Testament unexpurgated. After a while, however, the embargo seemed to be raised for some reason or other, and again I was allowed to revel with a great deal of profit in the wonderful poems, prophecies, and histories of the Old Testament. I soon discovered that it was impossible to understand the allusions in English literature without a knowledge of the Bible. What would "Ruth among the alien corn" mean to a reader who had never known the beauty of the story of Ruth? And the lilies of the field, permeating all poetical literature, would have lost all their perfume if one knew nothing about the Song of Solomon.

Putting aside the question as to whether young readers should be let loose in the Old Testament or not, or whether modern ideas of purity are justified in including ignorance as the supremest virtue, he who does not make himself familiar with Biblical ideas and phraseology finds himself in after-life with an incomplete medium of expression. It used to be said of the typical English gentleman that all he needed to know was to ride after the hounds and to construe Horace. This is not so absurd, after all, as it appears to be to most moderns. To construe Horace, of course, meant that he should have at least a speaking acquaintance with one of the masterpieces of Roman literature, and this knowledge gave him a grip on the universal speech of all cultivated people. However useless his allusions to Chloë and to Mæcenas were in the business of practical life, he was at least able to understand what they meant, and even a slight acquaintance with the Latins stamped him as speaking the speech of a gentleman.

Similarly, a man who knows the Scriptures is fitted with allusions that clarify and illuminate the ordinary speech. He may not have any technical knowledge, or his technical knowledge may be so great as to debar him from meeting other men in conversation on equal grounds; but his reading of the Bible gives his speech or writing a background, a colour, a metaphorical strength, which illuminate even the commonplace. Strike the Bible from the sphere of any man's experience and he is in a measure left out of much of that conversation which helps to make life endurable.

Pagan mythology is rather out of fashion. Even the poets often now assume that Clytie is a name that requires an explanation and that Daphne and her flight through the laurel do not bring up immediate memories of Syrinx and the reeds. The Dictionary of Lamprière is covered with dust; and one may quote an episode from Ovid without an answering glance of comprehension from the hearer. This does not imply ignorance; it is only that, in the modern system, the old mythology is not taken very seriously.

Since Latin and Greek have almost ceased to be a necessary part of a gentleman's education, there is no class of allusions from which we can draw to lighten or strengthen ordinary speech unless we turn to the Bible. This deprives conversation of much of its colour and renders it rather commonplace and meagre. Unfortunately, among many of our young people, the Bible seems to be a book to be avoided or to be treated in a rather "jocose" manner. To raise a laugh on the vaudeville stage, a Biblical quotation has only to be produced, and the weary comedian, when he is at a loss to get a witty speech across the footlights, is almost sure to speak of Jonah and the whale!

It is disappointing to notice this gradual change that has taken place in the attitude of the younger generation toward the Sacred Book. The Sunday Schools, in their attempt to make the genealogies of importance and to overload the memories of their little disciples with a multitude of texts, or to over-explain every allusion in the terms of physical geography, etc., may in a measure be responsible for this, but they cannot be entirely responsible. One must admit that diversities of interpretations of the Sacred Scriptures from a religious point of view will always be an obstacle to their use in schools where the children of Jews, of Mohammedans, and of the various Christian denominations assemble. But there is always the home, where the first impetus to a satisfactory knowledge of the Sacred Book ought to be given. The decay of the practice of reading aloud in our homes is very evident in the lack of real culture—or, rather, rudiments of real culture—in our children. But there is no use in declaiming against this. Other times, other manners; accusatory declamation is simply a luxury of Old Age!

Personally, my desultory reading of the Old and the New Testaments gave me a background against which I could see the trend of the books I devoured more clearly; it added immensely to my enjoyment of them; besides, it was a moral and ethical safeguard. It was easy even for a boy to discover that the morality of the New Testament was the standard by which not only life, but literature, which is the finest expression of life, should be judged. If there are great declamations, declamations full of dramatic fire, which nearly every boy at school learns to love, in the Old Testament, there are the most moving, tender, and simple stories in the New. To the uncorrupted mind, to the unjaded mind, which has not been forced to look on books as mere recitals of exciting adventures, the Acts of the Apostles are full of entrancing episodes. It is very easy for a receptive youth to acquire a taste for St. Paul, and I soon learned that St. Paul was not only one of the greatest of letter writers, but as a figure of history more interesting than Julius Cæsar, and certainly more modern. Young people delight in human documents. They may not know why they delight in these documents, but it is because of their humanity. Now who can be more human than St. Paul? And the more you read his epistles, and the more you know of his life, the more human he becomes. He knew how to be angry and sin not, and the way he "takes it out" of those unreasonable people who would not accept his mission has always been a great delight to me!

Under the spell of his writing, it was a pleasure to pick out the phases of his history—a history that even then seemed to be so very modern, and to a boy, with an unspoiled imagination, so very real. It seemed only natural that he should be converted by a blast of illumination from God. It is not hard for young people to accept miracles. All life is a miracle, and the rising and setting of the sun was to me no more of a miracle than the conversion of this fierce Jew, who was a Roman citizen. He seemed so very noble and yet so very humble. He could command and plead and weep and denounce; and he made you feel that he was generally right. And then he was a tentmaker who understood Greek and who could speak to the Greeks in their own language.

Late in the seventies when nearly every student I knew was a disciple of Huxley and Tyndal and devoted to that higher criticism of the Bible which was Germanizing us all, I fortified myself with St. Paul, and with the belief that, if he could break the close exclusiveness of the Jews, and take in the

Gentiles, if he could throw off, not contemptuously, many of the rigid ceremonies of his people, Christianity, in the modern time, could very well afford to accept the new geological interpretation of the story of Genesis without destroying in any way the faith which St. Paul preached.

Somewhat later, too, when I read constantly and with increasing delight the letters of Madame de Sévigné, I put her second as a writer of letters to the great St. Paul. The letters of Lord Chesterfield to his sons came next, I think; long after, Andrew Lang's "Letters to Dead Authors," and a very great letter I found in an English translation of Balzac's "Le Lys dans la Vallée."

It must not be understood that I put St. Paul in the same category with these mundane persons. Nevertheless, I found St. Paul very often reasonably mundane. He preferred to work as a tentmaker rather than take money from his clients, and one could imagine him as preaching while he worked. He frankly made collections for needy churches, and he was very grateful to Phœbe for remembering that he was a hungry man and in need of homely hospitality. He was interested in his fellow passengers Aquilla and Priscilla whom he met on board the ship that was taking them from Corinth to Ephesus. It was evident that they had not been able to make their salt in Corinth, where, however, their poverty had not interfered with their zeal in the cause of Christ. Any tent marked "Ephesus" was sure to have a good sale anywhere. The tents from Ephesus were as fashionable as the purple from Tyre, and St. Paul was pleased that his two disciples should have a chance of being more prosperous. I always felt, too, that, in his practical way, he knew that Ephesus would give him a better chance of supporting himself.

That Saul of Tarsus had not lacked for luxuries in his youth, one easily guessed. It was plain, too, that he had had the best possible instructors, and I liked to believe, when I was young, that his muscles had been well trained in the sports of gentlemen of his class. Altogether, so graphic were his descriptions and so potent his personality that, while Julius Cæsar and Brutus receded, he filled the foreground, and all the more because at this time I picked up an English translation of Suetonius, just by chance one dark winter day, and as I had not yet discovered that Suetonius was a "yellow" gossip, my idols, some of the Roman heroes, received a great shock.

The constant reading of St. Paul led me to the Acts of the Apostles, and I found St. Luke very good reading, though I often wished that, as I understood he had some reputation as an artist, he had adorned his writings with illustrations.

It was a great shock to discover that none of the Apostles wrote in English, for it seemed to me that their styles were as different from one another as any styles could be, and as I, having lived a great part of my time in classes where Nepos and Cæsar were translated by my dear young friends, had very little confidence in the work of any translator, I came to the conclusion that God had taken special care of the translators of the Bible, for I could not help believing that He had no interest whatever in the translations which we made daily for the impatient ears of our instructors!

One could not help loving St. Paul, too, because he was such a good fighter. When he said he fought with beasts, I was quite sure that these beasts were the unreasonable and unrighteous persons who persecuted and contradicted him. No obstacle deterred him, and he was gentle, too, although he called things by their right names and his denunciations were so vivid and mouthfilling that you knew his enemies must have been afraid to open their lips while he was near them, whatever they might have said behind his back.

My devotion to St. Paul brought me into disrepute one Friday at school when discipline was relaxed, and the teacher condescended to conversation. We were asked who was our favourite hero, and when it came to my turn I answered "St. Paul." As George Washington, Abraham Lincoln, Thomas Jefferson, General Grant, General Lee, Napoleon, and Alexander the Great, had walked in procession before I produced my hero, I was looked on as rather weakminded. The teacher, too, seemed astonished, and he asked me on what grounds I founded my worship. This question, coming suddenly, petrified me for a moment, and I answered, "He fought with beasts." This was taken as a personal allusion by some of my dear comrades with whom I had had altercations, and I was made to suffer for it as much as these dear comrades deemed prudent. However, they discovered that I had "language" on my side, for on the next composition day, when we read aloud the work of our brains, I accused them of "being filled with all iniquity," and other evil things which brought down a horrified remonstrance from the teacher, who was unaccustomed to such plain English, but he was knocked high and dry by the proof that I was only quoting St. Paul to the Romans.

Perhaps I became too familiar with St. Paul. Be that as it may, I regarded him as a very good friend indeed, for some of his "language," quoted in times of crisis, produced a much better effect on one's enemies than any swear word that could be invented. I am not excusing my attitude toward the Bible, but merely explaining how it affected my youthful mind. There was something extremely romantic in the very phrase, "the tumult of the silversmiths" at Ephesus. It seemed to mean a whole chapter of a novel in itself.

And there was the good centurion—Christ always seemed to have a sympathy for soldiers—who was willing to save Paul when the ship, on its way to Rome, was run aground. So he reached Melita where the amiable barbarians showed him no small courtesy. And one could not help liking the Romans; that is, the official Romans, even Felix, whose wife was a Jew like St. Paul, and who, disgusted when the Apostle spoke to him of chastity and of justice to come, yet hoped that money would be given him by Paul, and frequently sent for, and often spoke with him. And how fine seemed the Apostle's belief in his nobility as a Roman citizen! He rendered unto Cæsar the things that were Cæsar's. And one could easily imagine the pomp and circumstance when Agrippa and Bernice entered into the hall of audience with the tribunes and principal men of the city! And one could hear St. Paul saying, protecting himself nobly, through the nobility of a Roman law:

For it seemeth to me unreasonable to send a prisoner and not to signify the things laid to his charge,

and Agrippa's answer, after Paul's apologia:

In a little thou persuadest me to become a Christian!

But the story did not end then. I rehearsed over and over again what the King Agrippa might have said to his sister, the noble and beautiful Bernice— I knew nothing of the lady's reputation then—and how finally they did become Christians. In my imagination, princely dignity and exquisite grace were added to the external beauty of religion; and Paul went to Rome protected by the law of the Romans. And yet the very fineness of his attitude was the cause of his further imprisonment. "This man," I often repeated with Agrippa, "might have been set at liberty, if he had not appealed to Cæsar."

It was St. Paul who sent me back to the Prophet Micheas, who had previously struck me as of no importance at all, and I read:

And Thou, Bethlehem Ephrata, art a little one among the thousands of Juda; out of thee shall he come forth unto me that is to be the ruler in Israel; and his going forth is from the beginning, from the days of eternity.

And back again to St. Matthew—

But they said to him: In Bethlehem of Juda; For so it is written by the prophet; And thou, Bethlehem, the land of Juda, art not the least among the princes of Juda; for out of thee shall come forth the captain, who shall rule my people Israel.

These exercises in completing the prophecies of the Old Testament with the fulfilments of the New were interesting, and I found great pleasure in them. And this led me to a greater appreciation of the Old Testament, against which I had been once rather prejudiced. One day, I was led, by some reference or other in another book, to read the twenty-third psalm of David, in the King James version. It struck me as much more simple and appealing than the version in the Douai Bible, which begins in Latin "*Dominus regit me*." It runs:

The Lord ruleth me: and I shall want nothing.

2 He hath set me in a place of pasture.

He hath brought me up, on the water of refreshment:

3 He hath converted my soul. He hath led me on the paths of justice, for his own name's sake.

4 For though I should walk in the midst of the shadow of death, I fear no evils, for thou art with me.

Thy rod and thy staff, they have comforted me.

5 Thou hast prepared a table before me, against them that afflict me.

Thou hast anointed my head with oil: and my chalice which inebriateth me how goodly is it.

And thy mercy will follow me all the days of my life.

And that I may dwell in the house of the Lord, unto length of days.

In the Douai version this psalm was called the twenty-second.

Without any special guidance—I think most of my teachers would have looked on as dangerous any attempt to ally English literature with the Bible—I soon discovered that nearly everything I read owed something to the Bible. At first, the comparison of the twenty-third psalm in the King James version enraptured me so much that I began to find fault with the Latinized phrases of the Vulgate in English. It was the fashion in the early seventies to be very Saxon in speech, especially in the little group at school interested in English literature. Street cars at this time were comparatively new in Philadelphia, and I think we reached the last extremity of Saxonism in speech when we spoke of them as "folk wains." The tide then turned toward the Latins; and I preferred the Book of Job and the story of Ruth in the Latinized version, because the words were more mouth filling, and because it was very difficult to translate everything into a bald "early English medium", which for a time I had been trying to do. It was Keats's lovely phrase "amid the alien corn" which sent me back to "Ruth"; and a quotation in Quackenbos's "Rhetoric"—"Can'st thou hook the Leviathan" which made me revel in "Job."

Something Meg Merrilies said bore me on toward the roaring storm of Isaiah. The Latinized medium seemed to suit his denunciations best; and then, besides, I found more illuminating footnotes in the Douai version than in the King James. In both versions, some passages were so obscure that I often wondered how anybody could get any meaning out of them. I was often astonished to find in English novels that the old people in the cottages were soothed by texts, quoted at a great length, out of which I could make nothing, so I limited myself to the Douai version, which I found more illuminating.

Whether my system of reading is to be commended or not to young persons, I am not prepared to say, but for me it made the Bible a really live book. To be frank, and perhaps shocking at the same time—if anybody had asked me whether, being marooned on an island, I should have most preferred the Bible in my loneliness, I should promptly have answered "No." At this age "Nicholas Nickleby" or "Midsummer Night's Dream," or "The Tempest," or "As You Like it," or Macaulay's "Lays of Ancient Rome," would have suited me better, provided, of course, that I could have chosen only one book.

It was borne in on me many times that no author could improve on the phrasing of the Bible. Both in the Vulgate and the King James versions there are passages which, leaving aside all question of doctrine, it is sacrilege to try to improve. The French translation of the Bible is, as everybody knows, very paraphrastic, and that may account for the fact that, while regarded as a precious depository of doctrine, it is not a household book, and the dreadfully dull interpretations of Clement Marot—called hymns—naturally bored a people who, in their hearts, believe that God listens more amiably to petitions uttered in the language of the Academy! In their novels, dealing with the beginnings of Christianity—and there are many such novels in French unknown in other countries—it is hard for a French author not to be rhetorical, in the manner of the writer of "Ben Hur" when the death of Christ is described. No human author could improve on the words of the Vulgate, or the words of the King James version. What young heart can ponder over these words, without a thrill, St. John XIX (Douai version: 1609; Rheims; 1582):

When Jesus therefore had seen his Mother and the disciple standing whom he loved, he saith to his Mother: Woman, behold thy son.

After that, he saith to the disciple, Behold thy mother. And from that day the disciple took her to his own.

Afterwards, Jesus knowing that all things were now accomplished, that the Scripture might be fulfilled, said: I thirst.

Now there was a vessel set there full of vinegar, and they, putting a sponge full of vinegar about hyssop, put it to his mouth.

And Jesus therefore when he had taken the vinegar, said, it is consummated, and bowing his head, gave up the ghost.

When Marie Corelli became a popular author, there were persons existing—happily, they have all gone to the great beyond—who thought that the "talented" author could have done better!

Essays and Essayists

I am aware that many persons look on Emerson as somewhat dangerous reading for a boy of sixteen. The mothers and fathers of my Baptist friends and the uncle of my Methodist cousins forbade the reading of Emerson because of his Unitarianism; but, as the rector of our parish never denounced Unitarians from the altar, though he frequently offered his compliments to Martin Luther, I paid no attention whatever to these objections. I trust that I am not defending the miscellaneous reading of my boyhood; I do not recommend this course to the approval of parents and guardians; I am simply expressing the impression that certain books made on my youthful mind and heart; for, though I never said so in words, the books I liked were always nearer to my heart than to my mind. I owe a great debt to Emerson.

It was on a hot afternoon during the summer vacation that, near sundown, sitting on the warm marble steps of our house, I dipped into an early edition of Emerson. I felt inspired at once to think great thoughts and to do good things, to lift myself above the petty things of the earth, and to feel that to be an American was to be at once proud and humble. Emerson's abrupt sentences, like a number of brilliants set close together, reminded me of "Proverbs"; but the Book of Proverbs did not get so near to my actual life as the essays of Emerson. I liked the lessons that he drew from the lives of great men. I was shocked when he mentioned Confucius and Plato in the same breath as Christ; but I was amiably tolerant, for I felt that he had never had the privilege of studying the Little Catechism, and I thought of writing to him on the subject. But somebody told me that he was an "American Classic" and, from that, I concluded he was dead, and had doubtless already found out his mistake.

Perhaps I might have been better engaged in reading the more practical books offered to boys in our own time, if we had had them. There were some books then on scientific subjects, reduced to the comprehension of the young; but not so many as there are now. One of my uncles recommended the works of Samuel Smiles—"Self-Help" I think was his favourite; but Samuel Smiles never appealed to me. My small allowance, paid weekly, could not have been affected by "Thrift", and when my uncle quoted passages from this tiresome book I astounded him by replying, in a phrase I wrongly attributed to the adorable Emerson, that if I had a quarter to spend instead of twelve cents, I would give half of it for a hyacinth! My miserly uncle said it sounded just like Mohammed, and that Emerson had doubtless found it in that dangerous book, the Koran.

I cannot imagine any other author doing for me just what the essays of Emerson did. In the first place, they seemed to me to be really American; in the second, and largely because of their quality, they offered an antidote to the materialism in the very air, which had succeeded the Civil War. At this time there was much talk of money and luxury everywhere about us. Even in our quiet neighbourhood, where simple living was the rule, many had burst into ostentation, and moved away into newer and more pretentious quarters, and there was a rumour that some of these sought unlimited opportunities for extravagant expenditure. We saw them driving in new carriages, and condescendingly stopping before the white doors and the green window-shutters of our old-fashioned colonial houses. They had made money through the war. For the first time in our lives we boys heard of money making as the principal aim of life. The fact that these successful persons were classed as "shoddy" did not lessen the value of the auriferous atmosphere about us. Emerson was a corrective to this materialism. As to his philosophy or theology, that did not concern me any more than the religious opinions of Julius Cæsar, whose "Commentaries" I was obliged to read. Emerson gave me a taste for the reading of essay.

By chance I fell upon some essays of Carlyle. The inflation of his style did not deter me from thoroughly enjoying the paper on "Novalis." That on "Cagliostro," however, was my favourite. It introduced me intimately to the French Revolution. I disliked this great charlatan for his motto, "Tread the lilies under foot." I was for the Bourbons! The French Revolution, as a fact, was very near to me. My mother had been born (in Philadelphia) in 1819, and my great-uncle and my grandfather had lived through the French Revolution. There was a legend, moreover—probably the same legend exists in every family of Irish descent whose connections had lived in France—that one of them had been a clerk to Fabre d'Eglantine, and had spent his time in crossing off the list of the condemned the names of the Irish-French aristocrats and substituting in their place others that did not happen to belong to Celts!

In spite of the Little Catechism and the uplifting influence of Emerson, I looked on this probably mythical gentleman as one of the glories of our family. And then there was an old man—very old—who walked up and down Sixth Street with his head wrapped in a bandanna handkerchief, bearing a parrot on his shoulder. The boys of the neighbourhood believed that he was Sanson, the executioner of Louis XVI. and Marie Antoinette. We shivered when we saw him; but we boasted of his existence in our neighbourhood, all the same. After I had read "Cagliostro" I devoured every line on the subject of the French Revolution I could find. It seemed to me that I would have been willing to give five years out of my life to have lived in Paris during those horrors, and to have rescued Marie Antoinette and the Princess Elizabeth! Such brutalities seemed impossible in our time; and yet I have since lived very near to friends who went through even greater horrors in

Russia—the Baroness Sophie de Buxhoevenden, second lady-in-waiting to the Czarina, for instance, whose letters lie before me as I write.

In spite of my taste for Carlyle, which induced me to dip into Jean Paul Richter, of whose writings I remember only one line,

I love God and little children,

I did not get very far into his "French Revolution." It seemed then an unreal and lurid book.

Emerson led to Montaigne, whose essays, in an old edition which I had from the Mechanics' Institute, of which my father was a committeeman, delighted me beyond words. I liked Emerson's essay on "Friendship" better than his, but for wit, quick repartee, general cheerfulness, he reminded me of my favourite heroine in literature, Sir Walter Scott's Catherine Seton! Later, I read with astonishment that Montaigne was an unbeliever, a skeptic, almost a cynic. I was extremely indignant; he seemed to me to be a very pious gentleman, with that wit and humour which I seldom found in professedly pious books; and to this day I cannot hear Montaigne talked of as a precursor of Voltaire without believing that there is something crooked in the mind of the talker. So much for the impressions made in youth, so much for the long, long thoughts of which Longfellow sings.

Who is more amusingly cheerful than Montaigne, who more amusingly wise, who so well bred and attractive, who knew the world better and took it only as the world? Give me the old volume of Montaigne and a loaf of bread— no Victrola singing to me in the wilderness!—a thermos bottle, and one or two other things, and I can still spend the day in any wild place! I did not, of course, know, in those early days, what in his flavour attracted me. Afterward, I found that it was the very flavour and essence of Old France. Carlyle's impressions of historical persons interested me, but Montaigne was the most actual of living persons who spoke to me in a voice I recognized as wholly his. To be sure, I read him in Florio's translation.

I think it was about this time, too, that I discovered a very modern writer, who charmed me very greatly. It was Justin McCarthy who contributed a series of sketches of great men of the day to a magazine called the *Galaxy*. He "did" Victor Emmanuel and Pope Pius IX. and Bismarck, and many other of the worthies of the times. Nothing that he wrote before or after this pleased me at all; but these sketches were so interesting and apparently so true that they really became part of my life. If I had been asked at this time who was my favourite of all modern authors, and what the name of the composer I admired most, I should have said Justin McCarthy and Offenbach! I regarded "Voici le Sabre" in "La Grande Duchesse" as a masterpiece only to be compared to an "Ave Verum," by Pergolesi, which was often sung in St. Philip's Church at the Offertory! A strange mixture, but the truth is the truth. Although I have not been able to find Justin McCarthy's series of sketches, they still hold a sweet place in my memory. Perhaps, like other masterpieces that one loves in youth, one would now find them like those beautiful creatures of the sea that seem to be vermilion and purple and gold under the waves, but are drab and ugly things when taken out of the water. This applies to some books that one reads with pleasure in early days, and wonders, later, how they were endured!

There were not so many outdoor books in the late '60's as there are now. We were all sent to Thoreau's "Walden" and Dana's "Two Years Before the Mast." "Walden" I learned to like, but I much preferred Fenimore Cooper's description of nature. "Walden" struck me as the book of a man playing at out-of-doors, imagining his wildness, and never really liking to be too far from the town. Singularly enough, it was not until I discovered Hamerton's "A Painter's Camp" that I began to see that nature had beauties in all weathers. In truth, I hate to confess that nature alone never appealed to me. A landscape without human beings seemed deadly dull; and I did not understand until I grew much older that I had really believed that good art was an improvement on nature.

I have not the slightest idea in what light the modern critics see the works of Philip Gilbert Hamerton. I tried to read one of his novels recently, and failed; but let me say that, allowing for receptivity and what one may call temperament, I know of no book more revealing as to the relations of nature and art than "A Painter's Camp." I recall vividly the words of the beginning of the preface to the first edition:

It is known to all who are acquainted with the present condition of the fine arts in England that landscape-painters rely less on memory and invention than formerly, and that their work from nature is much more laborious than it used to be.

I had seen so many pictures that seemed to be "made up" in the artist's studio and I knew so well from my experience in the drawing classes at school, how nature was neglected for artificial models, that I hailed these words with great joy.

Everything in life was rather conventional, rather fixed, for the Centennial Exhibition in Philadelphia, to which our country owes the beginning of the æsthetic awakening, had not yet taken place. It may seem strange to this generation that we were limited to the wood-cuts in Godey's *Lady's Book*, the illustrations in *Harper's Magazine*, and an occasional picture in some short-lived periodical. The reign of the chromo had just begun. Rogers's groups were a fixture in nearly every self-respecting house, though I am glad to say, in my own family, very good casts of the Clytie and the Discus-thrower filled their place. My father greatly admired Power's Greek Slave, whose praises had been celebrated in the *Cosmopolitan Magazine*; but my mother regarded it as almost "improper."

Nearly every youth of my generation, in Philadelphia, wanted not exactly something better, but something more vivid. There were few sports; long walks and a little cricket supplied the place of the coming baseball and tennis.

In his "Steeplejack," James Huneker speaks of his weekly walks with Mr. Edward Roth, the head of a military school and the author of "Christus Judex." I, too, looked on these walks with an occasional row on the Schuylkill with him as the best part of my education. But this was later. All we could do, then, in our moments of leisure, was to walk and talk and read.

The cult of the out-of-doors had not yet begun to be developed. The beginning of "A Painter's Camp" was most attractive to my thirsty soul. Mr. Hamerton says:

I had a wild walk yesterday. I have a notion of encamping on the Boulsworth moors to study heather; and heartily tired of being caged up here in my library, with nothing to see but wet garden-walks and dripping yew trees, and a sundial whereon no shadow had fallen the livelong day, I determined, in spite of the rain to be off to the moors to choose a site for my encampment. Not very far from this house still dwells an old servant of my uncle's with whom I am on the friendliest terms. So I called upon this neighbour on my way and asked him if he would take a walk with me to the hills. Jamie stared a little and remarked that "it ur feefi weet" but accompanied me nevertheless, and a very pleasant walk we had of it.

Hamerton opened his book in Jane Eyre's country; our family had lately read "Jane Eyre." This added interest to the volume, and there came the details of the invention of the new hut, intended to be a shelter against all weathers, so that the artist might study nature on intimate terms. He made it in order to paint the heather at close range. Now, this was a revelation! It had never hitherto occurred to me that the heather changes its aspect day by day, or indeed that our pet place of beauty, the Wissahickon Creek, or river if you like, was not the same every day in the year except when the ice bound it! This may seem a rather stupid state of mind; but it is the stupidity that is very common. I could understand how interesting it would be to be in snow-fall while yet safely out of it. Mr. Hamerton thus described his hut:

It consists entirely of panels, of which the largest are two feet six inches square: these panels can be carried separately on packhorses, or even on men's backs, and then united together by iron bolts into a strong little building. Four of the largest panels serve as windows, being each of them filled with a large pane of excellent plate-glass. When erected, the walls present a perfectly smooth surface outside, and a panelled interior; the floor being formed in exactly the same manner, with the panelled or coffered side turned towards the earth, and the smooth surface uppermost. By this arrangement all the wall-bolts are inside, and those of the floor underneath it, which protects them not only from the weather but from theft, an iron bolt being a great temptation to country people on account of its convenience and utility. The walls are bolted to the floor, which gives great strength to the whole structure, and the panels are carefully ordered, like the stones in a well-built wall, so that the joints of the lower course of panels do not fall below those of the upper. The roof is arched and provides a current of fresh air, by placing ventilators at each end of the arch, which insures a current without inconvenience to the occupant.

The chapters on "Concerning Moonlight in Old Castles," "The Coming of the Clouds," and the little sketches, like "Loch Awe after Sunset, Sept. 23, 1860," enchanted me. It had not before struck me that Loch Awe was different on September 23, 1860, from what it was at other times, or—to carry the idea further—that the imperial Delaware had changed since that momentous time when George Washington crossed it, or the Schuylkill since Tom Moore looked upon it.

To quote further:

The mountain is green-grey, colder and greener towards the summit. All details of field and wood are dimly visible. Two islands nearer me are distinct against the hill, but their foliage seems black, and no details are visible in them. The sky is all clouded over. From the horizon to the zenith it is one veil of formless vapour.

And:

There is one streak of dead calm, which reflects the green mountain perfectly from edge to edge of it. There is another calm shaped like a great river, which is all green, touched with crimson. Besides these there are delicate half calms, just dulled over with faint breathings of the evening air; these, for the most part being violet (from the sky), except at a distance, where they take a deep crimson; and there is one piece of crimson calm near me set between a faint violet breeze and a calm of a different violet. There are one or two breezes sufficiently strong to cause ripple, and these rippled spaces take the dull grey slate of the upper sky.

Realise this picture as well as you may be able, and then put in the final touch. Between the dull calms and the glassy calms there are drawn thin threads of division burning with scarlet fire.

This fire is of course got from the lower sky. I know whence it comes, but how or why it lies in those thin scarlet threads there where it is most wanted, and not elsewhere, I cannot satisfactorily explain.

Then there was a delightful and illuminating chapter called "A Stream at Rest." Hamerton, who is probably now very much out of fashion, taught me the necessity of beauty in life; and, as an accessory to Emerson, the philosophy of enjoying the little, every-day things. It was Emerson who, I think, said first to me, "Take short outlooks"; and I still think that there can be no better introduction to a consideration of the relation of art to nature than "A Painter's Camp." It was "A Painter's Camp" which led me to "The Intellectual Life." There is a particular passage in Hamerton's chapter on "A Little French City" that emphasized the need of beauty.

The cathedral is all poetry; I mean that every part of it affects our emotional nature either by its own grandeur or beauty, or by its allusion to histories of bright virtue or brave fortitude. And this emotional result is independent of belief in the historical truth of these great legends: it would be stronger, no doubt, if we believed them, but we are still capable of feeling their solemn poetry and large significance as we feel the poetry and significance of "Sir Galahad" or "The Idylls of the King."

Some persons are so constituted that it is necessary to their happiness to live near some noble work of art or nature. A mountain is satisfactory to them because it is great and ever new, presenting itself every hour under aspects so unforeseen that one can gaze at it for years with unflagging interest. To some minds, to mine amongst others, human life is scarcely supportable far from some stately and magnificent object, worthy of endless study and admiration. But what of life in the plains? Truly, most plains are dreary enough, but still they may have fine trees, or a cathedral. And in the cathedral, here, I find no despicable compensation for the loss of dear old Ben Cruacha.

There are some humorous and perhaps even comic passages in "The Intellectual Life"; these passages are unconsciously humorous or comic, as Mr. Philip Gilbert Hamerton seems to have no sense of humour. For instance, it was a great surprise to me to discover that poverty was unfavourable to the intellectual life! It was enlightening to know the reason why a man should wear evening dress after six o'clock, and why the sporting of gray clothes in the evening was unworthy of the Intellectual! Besides, it affects the character!

And letter XI "To a Master of Arts who said that a Certain Distinguished Painter was Half-educated," was a useful antidote to youthful self-conceit. I had not reached the stage, treated in the chapters on "Women and Marriage," "To a Young Gentleman Who Contemplated Marriage," but I thought the author very wise indeed, and found many other pages which were intensely stimulating. Let others decry Hamerton if they like; I owe a great deal to him; and, though I might be induced to throw "The Intellectual Life" to the Young Wolves of the Beginning of this Century, I shall always insist that "A Painter's Camp" ought to be included in every list of books.

It was George Eliot who sent me to "The Following of Christ," and she interested me in Saint Teresa, that illustrious woman so well compounded of mysticism and common sense, of whom, however, I could find no good "Life." But Thomas à Kempis was a revelation! He fitted into nearly every crisis of the soul, but all his words are not for every-day life. He seems to demand too much of us poor folk of the world. Later, I came to understand that the counsel of perfection which Christ gave to the rich young man was not intended for the whole world, and many fine passages in À Kempis were meant for finer temperaments than my own.

Somebody at this time presented me with a copy of Marcus Aurelius. I found him dull, stale, and unprofitable in comparison with À Kempis. His philosophy of life seemed to lead to nothing except the cultivation of a very high opinion of oneself. I gave this conclusion to one of my English friends, who objected to my uncharted course of reading, and he said, "A person like you who finds nothing humorous or even philosophical in 'Alice in Wonderland' cannot be expected to like the works of Marcus Aurelius!"

It takes a prig to divide his reading into nicely staked off little plots, each with its own date. The art of injudicious reading, the art of miscellaneous reading which every normal man ought to cultivate, is a very fine and satisfactory art; for the best guide to books is a book itself. It clasps hands with a thousand other books. It has always seemed to me that "Sesame and Lilies" would not have been conceived by Ruskin if he had not heard well an echo of "The Following of Christ." There was a time when the lovers of Ruskin who wanted to read "The Stones of Venice" and the rest at leisure, felt themselves obliged to form clubs, and to divide the expense, if they were of moderate means, in order to get what was good out of him. But somehow or other, probably because it appealed more to everybody, it was always possible to find a copy of "Sesame and Lilies" at an old book stand. I think I found one most unexpectedly at Leary's in Philadelphia, where I also discovered the copy of Froissart. The Froissart, as I have said, cost me just half of my father's Christmas present that year, which was five dollars. I must have managed to get the Ruskin volume out of some other fund, for I had many things to buy with the other two and one half dollars!

Ruskin is left alone to-day; he does not seem to fill that "long-felt want" which we, the young of the sixties and seventies, admitted. No doubt he is very mannered in his style, mitred and coped when he might have been very simple in his raiment. He was a priest in literature and art; and he clothed himself as a priest. He marched with a stately tread, and yet he stooped to the single violets by the wayside.

By the way, I often wished when I was reading Ruskin, who once made apple blossoms fashionable, that he had led a crusade against the double and the triple violet, which have destroyed the reputation of the real violet. What can be more repellent to the lovers of simplicity than a bunch of these artificialities, without perfume, tied by dark green ribbon, and with all their leaves removed? "Sesame and Lilies" had the effect of sending me back to the single violet whenever I was inclined to admire the *camellia japonica* or any other thing that was artificial, or distorted from beauty or simplicity.

Circumstances have a great deal to do with our affection for books. Propinquity, they say, leads very frequently to marriage, and if a book happens to be near and if it is any kind of book at all, there is a great temptation to develop an affection for it. All I can say is that I think that "Sesame and Lilies" is a good book, for after all a book must be judged by its effect. It led me further into Ruskin, and helped me to acquire a reverence for art and to estimate the relations of art and life. One would steel oneself against the fallacy that art, true art, might exist only for art's sake, when one had read "Sesame and Lilies" and "The Stones of Venice." Those wise men who make literary "selections" for the young have done well to include in their volumes that graphic description, so carefully modulated in tone, of the Cathedral of St. Mark. Its only fault is that it comes too near to being prose poetry; and discriminating readers who ponder over it will find some epithets possible only to a writer who was an artist in lines and pigments before he began to paint with the pen.

Ruskin opened our eyes rather violently to some aspects of life which we, the young, did not know; for the young after all learn very little by intuition. They must be taught things. This is perhaps an excuse for those vagaries in youth, those seemingly inexplicable adventures which shock the old who have forgotten what it is to be young.

CHAPTER II

POETS AND POETRY
France—Of Maurice de Guérin

In 1872, the attention of readers was forced on a few great names. These were generally the names of Frenchmen. The sympathy of Americans during the Franco-Prussian War had been with France, and during the latter days of the French Empire, before the war, Americans had been much more interested in France than in any other part of the world. There were letters from Paris in the newspapers. The Empress Eugénie and her coterie at the Tuileries, the Operas of Offenbach, and the gossip about literary magnets of the time, which included a great deal of Victor Hugo, had been a constant subject of conversations.

One could buy French books easily in Philadelphia; and the Mercantile Library—now dreadfully shorn of its former pretensions, reduced in size, no longer so comfortable, so delightfully easy of access as to its shelves—had an excellent collection of volumes in French.

How often in later life I blessed the discriminating collectors of that library! Nothing worth while at that time, even "L'Homme" of Ernest Hello, seemed to have been left out; I fear that I was not always guided by the critics of the period. I found Amédée Achard as interesting as Octave Feuillet; George Sand bored me; I could never get through even "La Petite Fadette," although the critics were constantly recommending her for her "vitality." I found Madame de Gérardin's "La Femme qui Déteste Son Mari" one of the cleverest plays I had yet read. I have not seen it since; but, outside of some of the pieces of Augier, it seemed to me to be the best bit of construction I knew, and the human interest and the suspense were so admirably kept up. There were some plays by Octave Feuillet—"Redemption" was one and "Le Roman d'un Jeune Homme Pauvre," which divided my admiration with the management of "Adrienne Lecouvreur," by Scribe, and "Mademoiselle de la Seiglière," by Jules Sandeau. The French playwrights of to-day have not even the technique of their predecessors.

At this time I was very royalist, an infuriated partisan of the Comte de Chambord—Henry V., as a few of us preferred to call him. And this reminds me of my partisanship in things English—if I may turn for the moment from things French—and of a little incident not without humour. I was ardently devoted to the cause of the Stuarts, and was for a time attached to the White Rose Society, whose correspondents in England invariably sent their letters, with the stamp turned upside down, to indicate their contempt for the Guelf dynasty. But when, at a small and frugal reunion at Mr. Green's restaurant in

Philadelphia, our host—he was an American Walsh of the family of de Serrant—insisted on waving his glass of beer over the finger bowls, to insinuate that we were drinking to the last of the Stuarts across the water—whoever he might be—and another member suggested that, if it were not for the brutal Hanoverians on the throne of England, we, in the British Colonies, might be still enjoying the blessedness of being ruled by a descendant of Mary Stuart, I resigned! I was still devoutly faithful to the divine Mary of Scotland; but I would not have her mixed up in American politics!

Octave Feuillet satisfied my taste for elegance. Some of his people were not above reproach—notice the lady in "Redemption," who becomes suddenly converted to a belief in God because her twenty-fifth lover is suddenly restored to her. I thought that, though he was somewhat corrupted by the influence of the Tuileries, he was socially so admirably correct.

Everybody at this time talked of Renan. This went by me as an idle dream, for I could never understand why anybody should take a man seriously who was palpably wrong. To-day, when Renan's "Life of Jesus" seems almost forgotten, it is strange to recall the fury of interest it excited in the seventies. Louis Veuillot interested me much more than Renan, whom I avoided deliberately because I understood that he had attacked the Christian religion. Now, Louis Veuillot, in "Les Odeurs de Paris" and "Les Parfums de Rome" delighted me almost beyond bounds. I did often wonder how such a good man as Louis Veuillot could have acquired such un-Christian use of language. When he announced that if his wife wrote such novels as George Sand, he would hesitate to recognize her children, it seemed to me that he had gone too far—still it was a pleasant thing to shock the chaste Philadelphians by quoting these trenchant words when the novels of the lady in question were mentioned with rapt admiration.

But to come to the poets!

It was, I think, through the reading of the "Lundis" of Sainte-Beuve that I discovered Maurice de Guérin. He almost drove my beloved Keats from my mind. Somebody warned me against Maurice de Guérin on the ground of his pantheism. I had been warned against the poems of Emerson on account of their paganism; but as I had been brought up on Virgil, I looked on pantheism and paganism as rather orthodox compared to Renan's negation and the horrors of Calvinism. And, after all, the Catholic Church had retained so much that was Jewish and pagan that I was sure to find myself almost as much at home among the pagans as I was in the Old Testament at times.

Keats and Maurice de Guérin will be always associated in my mind. I discovered them about the same time. I had been solemnly told by an eminent Philadelphian that Wordsworth was the only poet worth considering, after Shakespeare, and that Keats had no intellectual value whatever. But I was not looking for intellectual value. I mixed up the intellect with a kind of scientific jargon about protoplasm and natural selection and the survival of the fittest, and bathybius, which was then all the fashion; so I promptly devoted myself to De Guérin.

I had already found great pleasure in the "Journal" of his sister Eugénie. The "Journal" ought never to be allowed to go out of fashion, and probably it is only out of fashion in those circles which Mr. Mencken so scorns, that devote themselves to imitations of Marie Bashkirtseff or Sarah McLean. I had begun to enjoy the flavour of the calm life of Eugénie at La Cayla when I found it necessary, in order to understand the allusions, to plunge again into the journals, letters, and poems of Maurice de Guérin. Thus it happened that I had fallen upon "Le Centaure" first. It is very short, as everybody knows. It was to me the most appealing poem I had ever read.

Keats's Greece seems somehow to be a Greece too full of modern colour, too unclassical. This was a mistake, of course, due to the fact that all my Greek reading had been filtered through professors and textbooks; and all my Greek seeing had been centred on pale white statues. It did not occur to me then—at least I did not know it—that the great Greek statues were not colourless, and that at Delphi there were statues that glowed with the hues of life. Strange to say, though "Le Centaure" seemed to me to be Greek in the classical sense, yet it palpitated with human emotion. Who that has read it can forget the simplicity of the opening? Says the Centaur:

I received my birth in the fastnesses of these mountains. As the stream of this valley of which the primitive drops run from the rocks which weep in a deep grotto, the first moment of my life fell among the darkness of a secluded place in which the silence was not troubled. When our mothers come near the time of their deliverance, they flee towards the caverns, and in the depth of the most remote, in the darkest of shadows, their children are born without a moan and the fruits of their womb are as silent as themselves. Their strong milk enables us to overcome without weakness or a doubtful struggle the first difficulties of life; however, we go out from our caves later than you from your cradles. It is understood among us that we must hide and envelope the first moments of existence as days filled by the gods. My growth followed its course almost among the shadows where I was born. The depth of my living place was so lost in the shadow of the mountain that I would not have known where the opening was if rushing sometimes into this opening the winds had not passed about me certain movements suddenly and refreshing breezes. Sometimes, too, my mother came back carrying the perfume of the valleys, or dripping with the waves of the water she frequented. Now these returns of hers gave me no knowledge of the valleys or the stream, but their suggestions disquieted my spirit, and I paced agitatedly in my shades.

After all, it requires leisure to enjoy fully the writings of Eugénie de Guérin and her brother—I inevitably think of this brother and sister together. There always lingers about the genius of these two delicate and sensitive beings a certain perfume of the white lilac which Maurice loved. It happened that through the amiability of my father, when I read the Journals of the De Guérins, I had leisure. A period of ill health stopped my work—I had begun to study law—and there were long days that could easily be filled by strolls in Fairmount Park in the early spring days, when it seems most appropriate to associate one's self with these two who ought to be read in the mood of the early spring, and they ought to be read slowly and even prayerfully. I hope I may be pardoned for quoting a sonnet which had a great vogue in the late 'seventies showing the impression that Maurice de Guérin made. It was a great surprise to find part of the sestette copied in the "Prose Writings" of Walt Whitman, who very rarely quoted any verse.

The old wine filled him, and he saw, with eyes
Anoint of Nature, fauns and dryads fair
Unseen by others; to him maidenhair
And waxen lilacs, and those birds that rise
A-sudden from tall reeds at slight surprise,
Brought charmèd thoughts; and in earth everywhere
He, like sad Jacques, found a music rare
As that of Syrinx to old Grecians wise.
A pagan heart, a Christian soul had he:
He followed Christ, yet for dead Pan he sighed,
Till earth and heaven met within his breast;
As if Theocritus in Sicily
Had come upon the Figure crucified
And lost his gods in deep, Christ given rest.

I found, too, satisfaction of the taste which Hamerton had corroborated, in Eugénie de Guérin's little sketches of outdoor scenery—sketches which always have a human interest. I had not yet begun to take any pleasure in Wordsworth; and, in fact, all the poets who seemed to be able to enjoy nature for itself—nature unrelieved or unimproved by human figures—had no attractions for me. And here the dear Edward Roth came in, and confirmed my taste. And there were heavy arguments with other clever Philadelphians, Doctor Nolan, the scientist who loved letters, and that amateur of literature, Charles Devenny.

As for Pope and his school, they seemed to represent an aspect of the world as unreal as the world of Watteau, and with much less excuse; but pictures of the kind I found in the "Journal" of Eugénie de Guérin had a living charm. At this time, I had not seen Matthew Arnold's paper on Maurice de Guérin, and I did not know that any appreciation of his sister had been written in English. I had seen a paragraph or two written by some third-rate person who objected to her piety as sentimental, and incomprehensible to the "Anglo-Saxon" world! That her piety should be sentimental, if Eugénie's sentiment can be characterized by that term, seemed to me to be questionable; and it was evident that any one who read French literature at all must be aware that there were hundreds of beautiful sentiments and phrases which the average "Anglo-Saxon" world found it impossible to comprehend.

The beloved home of Eugénie, La Cayla, was not a gay place. It was even more circumscribed than Miss Mitford's "Village"; but Eugénie, being less "Anglo-Saxon" than Miss Mitford, had more sentiment and a more sensitive perception of the meaning of nature—though, when it comes to sentimentalism, the English man or woman, who often masquerades under the shelter of "Anglo-Saxonism," is as sentimental as the most sentimental of sentimentalists. This is what I mean by the landscape charm of Eugénie de Guérin, and yet the picture in this case is not a landscape, but the interior of a room:

I was admiring just now a little landscape, presented by my room, as it was being illuminated with the rising sun. How pretty it was! Never did I see a more beautiful effect of light on the paper, thrown through painted trees. It was diaphanous, transparent. It was almost wasted on my eyes; it ought to have been seen by a painter. And yet does not God create the beautiful for everybody? All our birds were singing this morning while I was at my prayers. This accompaniment pleases me, though it distracts me a little. I stop to listen; then I begin again, thinking that the birds and I are alike singing a hymn to God, and that, perhaps, those little creatures sing better than I. But the charm of prayer, the charm of communion with God, they cannot enjoy that; one must have a soul to feel it. This happiness that the birds have not is mine. It is sorrow. How little time is needed for that. The joy comes from the sun, the mild air, the song of birds, all delights to me; as well as from a letter of Mimi's (who is now at Gaillac), in which she tells me of Madame Vialar, who has seen thee, and of other cheerful things.

And again:

However, I had a delightful waking this morning. As I was opening my eyes a lovely moon faced my window, and shone into my bed, so brightly that at first I thought it was a lamp suspended to my shutter. It was very sweet and pretty to look at this white light, and so I contemplated, admired, watched it till it hid itself behind the shutter to peep out again, and then conceal itself like a child playing at hide-and-seek.

Emerson tried to teach us that there can be infinite beauties in a little space—untold joys within a day—and he asks us to take short outlooks. Saint Teresa and Saint Francis de Sales were before him in this; but Eugénie de Guérin exemplifies its value much more than any other modern writer. Her soul was often sad, but it never ceased to find joy in the little happinesses of life. In our country, we are losing this faculty which the best of the later New Englanders tried to recover. It is a pity because it deprives us of the real *joie de vivre* which is not dependent on ecstasies of restless emotions or violent amusements.

The devotion of Eugénie de Guérin to her brother resembles that of Madame de Sévigné for her daughter, the peerless Pauline. It was George Sand who discovered the genius of that brother, though her characterization of the qualities of his genius did not please the Christian soul of his sister. It was left to Sainte-Beuve to fix De Guérin's place in French literature; and I recall now that the reading of Sainte-Beuve led me to find the poems of David Gray, now probably forgotten, and to go back to Keats.

After Maurice de Guérin's "Le Centaure" I found Keats even less Greek than I thought he was, because he was less philosophical than De Guérin, and because he did not concern himself with the gravest questions of life; but, after all, Keats is the poet for the poets!

My dear friend, Edward Roth—whom James Huneker celebrates in his "Steeplejack"—named Spenser as "the poet of the poets"; but Spenser is too hard to read—even harder than Chaucer, and certainly more involved, while no poets that ever lived can make pictures so glowing, so full of a sensitive and exquisite light as Keats. Later, it seemed absurd for the French poets of a certain *genre* to call themselves symbolists. When Keats wrote, he saw and felt, and he saw because he felt. It was not necessary for him to search laboriously for the colour of a word. The thing itself coloured the word—and Keats, working hard in a verbal laboratory, would have been an anomaly. It was not necessary for him to study carefully the music of his verse as Campion did or Coventry Patmore or as Sidney Lanier is supposed to have done—though one cannot have suspected that Sidney Lanier's elaborate laboratory was erected after his best verse had been written.

Maurice de Guérin, a very Christian soul, was probably disturbed in his religious sentiments by the defection of his old friend and director, Père de Lamennais—the "M. Féli" of the little paradise of la Chénie. To the delight of some of the more independent and emancipated of the literary circle at

Paris, which included George Sand, Maurice was becoming more pantheistic than Christian. He seemed to have tried to make for humanity an altar on which Christ and Nature might be almost equally adored, and this gave Eugénie great pain, although it did not change her love or make a rift in her belief in him.

De Guérin is a singing poet in a language which is used by few singing poets for serious themes. There are few lyric poems in French, like the "Chanson de Fortunio" of Alfred de Musset. It was not strange that the great Sainte-Beuve found the verse of De Guérin somewhat too unusual. Sainte-Beuve calls it "the familiar Alexandrine reduced to a conversational tone, and taking all the little turns of an intimate talk." Eugénie complains that "it sings too much and does not talk enough." However, one of the most charming of literary essays, to which Matthew Arnold's seems almost "common," is that preceding Trébutien's "Journals, Letters, and Poems of Maurice de Guérin." It would be folly for me to try to permeate the mind of any other person with the atmosphere which still palpitates in me when I think of the first delight of reading at leisure the poems of Maurice and the letters of Eugénie. I might just as well attempt to make a young man of our time feel the thrill that came when we were young and first heard the most beautiful of all love songs—"Come into the Garden, Maud!"

One can hear the amazed laughter, the superior giggles that would arise from a group of Greenwich Villagers if they did me the honour to read this page; but the real Quartier Latin has better taste and is not so imitative—and paraphrases of this lovely lyric still find admirers in the gardens of the Luxembourg and on the heights of Montmartre. Tennyson, like De Guérin, had bent the old classic form to newer usage, and one can hardly help seeing, in spite of the fact that the admirers of Swinburne claim this laurel for him, that Tennyson discovered the secret of making lyrical verse musical while discarding rime. Both Maurice de Guérin and Tennyson, who have superficial characteristics in common, send us back to Theocritus, the most human, the most lyrical, the most unaffectedly pagan of all the poets who wrote before Pan said his despairing good-bye to all the Grecian Isles. But what a mixture is this!—Maurice and Eugénie de Guérin, Keats, Madame de Sévigné, Theocritus, and Tennyson, the Elizabethan Campion—and yet they are all related.

In fact, ladies and gentlemen, I have never read any good book that was not related intimately to at least a score of other books. It is true that in a measure a book gives to us what we take to it; and we can only take much out of it when we approach the group of ministering authors who alone make life both cheerful and endurable.

The received methods of "teaching" the classics in what people call "the dead languages" nearly always weaken the faculties of the soul, while they may develop certain hidden abilities of the mind. This favourite process of pedagogues very often defeats itself. Mr. Edward Roth honestly believed that the Roman Empire had risen, declined, and fallen in order that the Latin language might live! The logical result of this teaching on the eager young mind, at once logical, ductile, and obstinate, was to induce it to discover something about the Roman Empire, in order that it might cease to yawn over the declensions, and to be bored by prosody; to discover why the glorious Empire had lived and died in order to produce an elaborate mound of charred bones! Mr. Roth himself, though a classicist of the classicists, managed to make the Romans interesting in conversation; he always impressed one that the Roman baths, or the chariot races, or the banquets, which he admitted were full of colour and life, were by comparison faded and pale in the glow and aroma of the sentences invented by the Latins to describe them!

The impossibility of getting anything out of the study of Greek by hard work, sent me, after I had read Maurice de Guérin's "Centaure," to read joyously an edition of the "Idyls of Theocritus" in French. While browsing I found on the shelves of the Mercantile Library the novels of Tourguéneff in the same language. This delayed me a little. I found Theocritus and Bion and Moschus in the Bohn Edition, which I think has now become the beneficent "Everyman's Library." I revelled! The Mimes of Herondas had not yet been discovered, but some of the dialogues in these poems contained all the best of their essences. My friends among the hard workers at the "Classics" scorned me. The elderly gentleman from Oxford who gave us lessons three or four times a week and held that, when we were able to translate at sight a certain page of Greek which he had composed himself from various great authors, that we were perfect, treated me as a pariah; but that made no difference. I continued, in merciful leisure, to saturate myself in the golden glow of the Sicilian poets. I tried hard to express my devotion to Theocritus by paraphrases, very slightly from the original Greek, mostly from the French, and partly from the Bohn Edition. I quote a result which Mr. Edmund Clarence Stedman said was too paraphrastic. It is from the "Cyclops":

Softer than lambs and whiter than the curds,
O Galatea, swan-nymph of the sea!
Vain is my longing, worthless are my words;
Why do you come in night's sweet dreams to me,
And when I wake, swift leave me, as in fear
The lambkin hastens when a wolf is near?

Why did my mother on a dark-bright day
Bring you, for hyacinths, a-near my cave?
I was the guide, and through the tangled way
I thoughtless led you; I am now your slave.
Peace left my soul when you knocked at my heart—
Come, Galatea, never to depart!

Though I am dark and ugly to the sight—
A Cyclops I, and stronger there are few—
Of you I dream through all the quick-paced night,
And in the morn ten fawns I feed for you,
And four young bears: O rise from grots below,
Soft love and peace with me forever know!

Last night I dreamed that I, a monster gilled,
Swam in the sea and saw you singing there:
I gave you lilies and your grotto filled
With the sweet odours of all flowers rare;
I gave you apples, as I kissed your hand,
And reddest poppies from my richest land.

Oh, brave the restless billows of your world:
They toss and tremble; see my cypress-grove,
And bending laurels, and the tendrils curled
Of honeyed grapes, and a fresh treasure-trove
In vine-crowned Ætna, of pure-running rills!
O Galatea, kill the scorn that kills!

Softer than lambs and whiter than the curds,
O Galatea, listen to my prayer:
Come, come to land, and hear the song of birds;
Rise, rise, from ocean-depths, as lily-fair
As you are in my dreams! Come, then, O Sleep,
For you alone can bring her from the deep.

And Galatea, in her cool, green waves,
Plaits her long hair with purple flower-bells,
And laughs and sings, while black-browed Cyclops raves
And to the wind his love-lorn story tells:
For well she knows that Cyclops will ere long
Forget, as poets do, his pain in song.

No sensitive mind can dwell on Theocritus, even when interpreted in English prose, without feeling something of the joy of the old Syracusan in life. His human nature is of the kind that makes the nymphs and swains of Alexander Pope dull and artificial. There are flies in this delicious ointment, one must admit, touches of corruption which a degenerate paganism condoned and palliated, but we must remember, as an extenuation of the Greek attitude, that the oracle of Delphi protested against them. The cyprus plains of Theocritus yet echo with the call of the cicada, and the anemones still bloom. The pipes of Pan are not all silent. The world would lose some of its beauty if Theocritus and the Sicilian poets did not entice us to hear their echoes.

But to how many links of a long chain does Maurice de Guérin lead us! Here is another link—José de Herédia, and his jewelled and chiselled sonnets—the "Antique Medal" with its peerless sestette, which combines the essential meanings of Keats's "Ode to a Grecian Urn."

Le temps passe. Tout meurt. Le marbre même s'use.
Argrigente n'est plus qu'une ombre, et Syracuse
Dort sous le bleu linceul de son ciel indulgent;

Et seul le dur métal que l'amour fit docile
Garde encore en sa fleur, aux médailles d'argent,
L'immortelle beauté des vierges de Sicile."

A translation of which reads:

Time goes; all dies; marble itself decays;
A shadow Agrigentum; Syracuse
Sleeps, still in death, beneath her kind sky's shades;
But the hard metal guards through all the days,
Silver grown docile unto love's own use,
The immortal beauty of Sicilian maids.

I always felt that Dante would have been less devoted to Virgil had he known Theocritus. The artificial Roman seems faded when one compares his rural elegies with the lovely pictures of the first of all the Syracusan poets. Horatius Flaccus had more of the quality of Theocritus than of Virgil; and though Virgil might have been a good guide for Dante in his sublime wanderings, he was a guide of the intellect rather than of the heart. It requires some courage, perhaps, to confess that one reads Theocritus in English rather than in Greek. The French rendering is too paraphrastic; but, although my classical friends, or rather my friends *enragé* of the "Classics," honestly despise me for making this confession, I shamelessly enjoy Theocritus in the Bohn Edition, without even using it as a "crib" to the forgotten Greek text rather than begin a course of Grecian philology and to lose the perfume of the crushed thyme or the sight of the competing shepherds on the shrub-dotted prairie.

Dante

A constant reader is one who always returns to his first loves. He may find them changed because he has changed; but the soul of that reader is dead who never goes back to "Ivanhoe" to renew the thrill of the famous tournament or to discover whether Leather Stocking is the superman he once seemed to be. I find myself, in old age, divided between two conflicting opinions. "There is no leisure in this country," I am told. "A great change has taken place. The motor car has destroyed the art of reading, and, as for the good old books—nobody reads them any more." On the other hand, I hear, "People do read, but they read only frivolous books which follow one another like the hot-cakes made at noon in the windows of Mr. Child's restaurants."

Personally, I cannot accept either opinion. In the first place, the winter is the time for reading—I recall Robert Underwood Johnson's "Winter Hour" when I think of this—and the motor car, especially in country places, does not function violently in the winter time. Many journeys from Boston, through New England, to the Middle West have taught me that folk are reading and discussing books more than ever. Whatever may be said of the mass of American people, who are probably learning slowly what national culture means, there are at the top of this mass thousands of Americans who love good books, who possess good books, and who return each year to the loves of their youth.

The celebration of the sixth centenary of the death of Dante Alighieri proves this. It is true enough that Dante and Goethe and Milton are more talked about in English-speaking countries than read, and when the enthusiasm awakened in honour of the great Florentine reached its height, there were found many people in our country who were quite capable of asking why Dante should be read.

Looking back I found it easy to answer this question myself, for, perhaps, beginning with a little gentle aversion to the English rimed translations of the "Divine Comedy," my love for Dante has been a slow growth. The Dante specialists discourage us with their learning. There are few who, like Mr. Plimpton, can lucidly expose the foundations of the educations of Dante to us without frightening us by the sight of a wall of impregnable erudition. Naturally, one cannot approach Dante in order to begin an education in the Middle Ages and the Renascence which one never began in one's own time; but to be consoled by Dante it is not necessary to be erudite. In fact, to the mind bent on spiritual enlightenment, the notes of the erudite, above all, the conjectures of the erudite, are frequently wrong. Even Israel Gollancz, in his three valuable volumes in the Temple Edition, nods over his notes occasionally. And by the way, for all amateurs in the reading of the "Divine Comedy" nothing can be better than this Temple Edition, which contains the Italian on one page and a lucid prose translation into English on the next. As I grew older I grew more and more enamoured of Longfellow's Dantean Sonnets, but not of his translation, for all rime translations must be one half, at least, the author and the other half the translator. Gollancz is best for anybody who does not enjoy poetic *tours de force*.

In his note on the most popular lines in the "Divine Comedy,"

Nessun maggior dolors,
che ricordarsi del tempo felice
nella miseria;

Gollancz says:

Although these words are translated literally from Boëthius, and although we know that Dante had made a special study of Boëthius, yet we cannot well identify the *dottore* with this philosopher: for how can we be expected to assume that Francesca was acquainted with these two facts? The reference is probably to Virgil, and to his position in Limbo.

Into this Limbo Christ descended fifty-two years after Virgil's death and drew certain souls up with him to Heaven. We are, however, by no means certain that Virgil was happier on earth than he was "upon the green enamel" (*verde smalto*) in this place of quiet leisure which was the vestibule to Hell, but not Hell itself, and which, to some chosen souls, had already been a vestibule to the Palace of the Beatific Vision. If Dante had been translated in the old days of rigid Calvinism in Scotland and New England, his tolerance of the pagans who found parts of Hell not entirely uncomfortable would have caused him to be looked on as a corruptor of the faith. But what would they have said to the "Paradiso" which I have always found more full of consolation than any sermon that was ever preached? Let us take the description of the Church Triumphant in Canto XXXII. How sweetly Dante disposes of the heresy that all children unbaptized by material water are doomed:

Dunque, senza merce di lor costume,
locati son per gradi differenti,
sol differendo nel primiero acume.

Bastava si nei secoli recenti
con l'innocenza, per aver salute,
solamente la fede dei parenti;

poiche le prime etadi fur compiute,
convenne ai maschi all' innocenti penne,
per circoncidere, acquistar virtute.

Ma poichee il tempo della grazia venne,
senza battesmo perfetto di Cristo,
tale innocenza laggiu si ritenne.

And then remembering the innocence of the little children Dante turns to that face "which is most likest unto Christ's" the face of Mary the Mother, who is the protectress and friend of all children. If the strict Calvinists had known the "Paradiso" of Dante as well as they knew their Old Testament, their theology might have found more adherence among the merciful, for the "Paradiso" is a triumphant song of mercy, of love, and of the final triumph of every soul that has sincerely hoped in, or sought, the truth, even if the truth were not crowned in its fullness in this world.

And Dante, put by Raphael without protest from the Church Militant, among the Doctors of the Faith, glorifies Trajan among the Saved and opens Heaven to Cato. This shows, by the way, the falsity of the Voltairean *mauvais mot*, that all the people worth meeting are in Hell! And Dante sees Constantine in Heaven, although he thinks that this Emperor's donation of territory was an evil gift. Dante, who, by the way, was nearer to the old records and this tradition of the older time, is a witness against Lord Bryce's assertion that the documents of Constantine's donation were mediæval forgeries. Dante believed, however, that the donation was invalid, because the successor of St. Peter, being of the spirit, could not accept temporal power. This he asserts in his "De Monarchia," which was for a time on the "Index." Times have changed, and "De Monarchia" and Milton's "Paradise Lost" are no longer in the "Index," though Balzac and Dumas, in French, are. But many of the Faithful in the United States console themselves by assuming that, as in the case of Dr. Zahm's "Religion and Science," this the method of the Sacred Congregation is not without its distinctions. Dr. Zahm's book, suppressed in Italian, received the proper "imprimatur" in English! So may "The Three Musketeers" and may "Monte Cristo" be regarded as coming under the ban in the original, but as tolerated in the translation?

Dante's bitterness against certain Popes made no rift in his creed, nor does it seem to have made him less respected by the Roman Court. There is in the "Paradiso" that great passage on the poet's faith—

Così spirò di quell' amore acceso;
indi soggiunse: "Assai bene è trascorsad'
esta moneta già la lega e il peso;

ma dimmi se tu l' hai nella tua borsa.
"ed' io: "Si, l'ho, si lucida e si tonda,
che nel suo conio nulla mi s' inforsa."

Appresso uscì della luce profonda,
che lì splendeva; "Questa cara gioia,
sopra la quale ogni virtù si fonda,
onde ti venne?" Ed io: "La larga ploia
dello Spirito Santo, ch' è diffusa
in su le vecchie e in su le nuove cuoia,

È sillogismo, che la mia ha conchiusa
acutamente sì, che in verso d' ella
ogni dimostrazion mi pare ottusa."

If the reading of the "Paradiso" turns one to other books, so much the better. Aristotle is worth while; he holds the germ of what is best in modern life; and St. Thomas Aquinas, his echo, with new harmonies added the Wagner to Aristotle's Mozart. No—that is going too far!—the musical comparison fails. "If thou should'st never see my face again, pray for my soul," is King Arthur's prayer. It is the prayer of Pope Gregory that saved Trajan.

When we come to the "Purgatorio," like the "Paradiso" too neglected, we find much that illuminates our minds and touches our hearts. The "Purgatorio" is not without humour, and it is certainly very human. For instance, there is the case of the negligent ruler, Nino de' Visconti. Dante is frankly pleased to meet him, but his address is hardly tactful. He is evidently surprised to find that Nino is not in Hell,

When he came near to me I said to him;
gentle Judge Nino, how I'm delighted well
that I have seen thee here and not in Hell.

Nino begs that his innocent daughter, Giovanna, may be asked by Dante, on his return to earth, to pray for him. He is not pleased that his widow should desire to marry

the Milanese who blazoned a viper on his shield.

He thinks that his wife has ceased to love him as she has discarded her "white wimples," which, if she marries this inferior person, she may long for once again! And he adds, rather cynically, for a blessed soul in Purgatory, that through her one may mightily well know how short a time love may last in woman, if the eye and the touch do not keep it alive.

One must admit that there is an element of humour—not for the victim—in the "Inferno," when Dante puts Pope Boniface VIII. into Hell three and a half years before he died! Nicholas III., whom Dante thought guilty of the unpardonable sin of simony, had preceded Boniface; and he says,

E se non fosse ch' ancor lo mi vieta
la riverenza delle somme chiavi,
che tu tenesti nella vita lieta
l' userei parole ancor più gravi—

But for consolation, there is no great poem so good as the "Paradiso."

English and American Verse

Edmund Clarence Stedman tells us how thrilled the youths of his generation were when the new poet, Tennyson, "swam into their ken." It is difficult for the young of to-day to believe this. There is no great reigning poet to-day; there are great numbers of fair poets, who are hailed as crown princes by the groups that gather about them. Whatever the old may say, this is a good sign. Any evidence of a sincere interest in poetry is a good sign. Tennyson's "Dream of Fair Women" and his portrait studies broke in on the old tradition. "The Lady of Shalott," with its pictures of silence and its fine transmutation of commonplace into something very beautiful, was new.

We who succeeded Stedman by some years loved all the beauty of Tennyson while we were not especially struck by those mediæval lay figures which he labelled "King Arthur" and "Sir Galahad" and "Sir Percival." They were too much like what the English people at that time insisted that the Prince Consort was. Even Sir Lancelot would have profited in our eyes by a touch of the fire of Milton's "Lucifer." But the lyricism of Tennyson, the music of Tennyson, is as real now as it was then. It is the desire for "independence," the fear of following a conventionality, a fear that calls itself audacity, which brushes away the delicate and scientific of this exquisite poet simply because he does not represent a Movement. And yet all these new movements are very old movements. The result of the education given me by books was to convince me that the man of culture proclaims himself third-rate if he looks on any literary expression as really new and if he cannot enjoy the old, when the old is of all time. The beautiful and the real can never be old or new because they are the same through the movement of time. To explain what I mean, let me come suddenly down to date and permit me to quote from Sir Arthur Quiller-Couch's "On the Art of Reading." He is writing of the Bible, which is never old:

I daresay, after all, that the best way is not to bother a boy too early and overmuch with history; that the best way is to let him ramp at first through the Scriptures even as he might through "The Arabian Nights": to let him take the books as they come, merely indicating, for instance, that Job is a great poem, the Psalms great lyrics, the story of Ruth a lovely idyll, the Song of Songs the perfection of an Eastern love-poem. Well, and what then? He will certainly get less of "The Cotter's Saturday Night" into it, and certainly more of the truth of the East. There he will feel the whole splendid barbaric story for himself: the flocks of Abraham and Laban; the trek of Jacob's sons to Egypt for corn; the figures of Rebekah at the well, Ruth at the gleaning, and Rizpah beneath the gibbet; Sisera bowing in weariness; Saul—great Saul—by the tent-prop with the jewels in his turban:

"All its lordly male-sapphires, and rubies courageous at heart."

Or consider—to choose one or two pictures out of the tremendous procession—consider Michal, Saul's royal daughter: how first she is given in marriage to David to be a snare for him; how, loving him, she saves his life, letting him down from the window and dressing up an image on the bed in his place; how, later, she is handed over to another husband Phaltiel, how David demands her back, and she goes:

"And her husband (Phaltiel) went with her along weeping behind her to Bahurim. Then said Abner unto him, Go, return. And he returned."

Or, still later, how the revulsion takes her, Saul's daughter as she sees David capering home before the ark, and how her affection had done with this emotional man of the ruddy countenance, so prone to weep in his bed:

"And as the ark of the Lord came into the city of David, Michal, Saul's daughter"—

Mark the three words—

"Michal, Saul's daughter looked through a window, and saw King David leaping and dancing before the Lord; and she despised him in her heart."

Mr. Galsworthy or Mr. W. L. George or Mr. Maxwell, who are rapidly becoming too old-fashioned for the young, or Mrs. Wharton, or Mrs. Gertrude Atherton would treat this episode in sympathy with what they might conceive to be the trend of present emotion; for it is with the emotions and not with the mind or the will that the novelist of the day before yesterday mostly deals. If Mr. James Huneker had translated this into the prose of his moment, it would have flamed with minutely carved jewels, glowed with a perfume and colour of crushed roses, and choked the reader with the odour of musk. But could he have made it any "newer"? Or if he could have made it "newer," could he have made it more splendid and appealing?

The old is new, and the new is old in art and literature—in life itself, and the man who scorned Keats because Swinburne and Rossetti were new; or who scorns Browning—the best of Browning—lacks the first requisite of true cultivation which is founded on the truth that beauty is beyond the touch of time. The women in François Villon's "Ballade of Dead Ladies" are gone, but their beauty remains in that song. This beauty might be none the less beautiful if expressed in *vers libre*; its beauty might take a new flavour from our time. The fact only that it was of our time and treated in the manner of our time, could not give it that essential and divine something which is perennial, universal, and perhaps eternal.

Much affectionate reading of poetry—and poetry read in any other way is like the crackling of small sticks under a pot in the open air on a damp day— leads one to consider the structure of verse and to ask how singing effects are best produced. This inquiry has led some of the sincerest of the younger poets to throw aside the older conventions, and, imitating Debussy, Richard Strauss, and even newer composers, to produce that "free verse" which, in the hands of the inexpert, the lazy, or the ignorant, becomes lawless verse. It is exasperating to the intolerant to find writers, young in experience if not always young in age, talking of themselves as discoverers—brave or audacious discoverers—as adventurers, reckless as Balboa, or Cortez, or Ponce de León; and then, to hear some of the old and conventional violently attacking these verse makers as if they were new and dangerous revolutionists.

The truth is that *vers libre* has its place, and it ought to have a high place; but the writer who attempts it must have a very perfect ear for the nuances of music and great art in his technique applied to the use of words. Some of the disciples of Miss Amy Lowell have this, but they are few. Whether Miss Lowell has mastered the science or not, she has the fine art of producing musical effects, delicate and various and even splendid. But there are others!

It may have been Tennyson, or Theocritus, or Campion that led me to read Coventry Patmore. I know that it was not his "The Angel in the House" which led me on. That seemed as little interesting or important as the proverbial sayings of Martin Farquhar Tupper; but one day I found "The Unknown Eros" and a little later "The Toys," and then his "Night and Sleep," one of the most musical poems in our language.

How strange at night the bay
Of dogs, how wild the note
Of cocks that scream for day,
In homesteads far remote;
How strange and wild to hear
The old and crumbling tower,

Amid the darkness, suddenly
Take tongue and speak the hour!

Although the music of "Night and Sleep" is not dependent upon the rime, it is plain—as the form of poetry appeals to the ear—that the rime is a gain. Yet one does not miss it in the fifth and seventh lines of each stanza. The real musical charm of the poem—only one stanza, of four, is given here—lies in the management of the rhythm.

We have only to fill up the measure in every line as well as in the seventh, in order to change this verse from the slowest and most mournful to the most rapid and high-spirited of all English, the common eight-syllable quatrain,

says Mr. Patmore in his "Essay on English Metrical Law,"

a measure particularly recommended by the early critics, and continually chosen by poets in all times for erotic poetry on account of its joyful air. The reason of this unusual rapidity of movement is the unusual character of the eight-syllable verse as acatalectic, almost all other kinds of verse being catalectic on at least one syllable, implying a final pause of corresponding duration.

Mr. Patmore here shows that the rime in this lovely "Night and Sleep" is merely accessory, a lightly played accompaniment to a song which would be as beautiful a song without it, yet which gains a certain accent through this accompaniment; and that the real questions in verse are of rhythm and time. Tennyson, whose technique, even in the use of sibilants, will bear the closest scrutiny, often proves the merely accessory value of rime, but in no instance more fully than in

Tears, idle tears, I know not what they mean,Tears from the depth of some divine despairRise in the heart and gather in the eyes,In looking on the happy autumn fields,And thinking of the days that are no more.

There is every reason why the modern reader should have become tired of academic poetry. When poetry divorced itself from music and became the slave of fixed rules of metre which could not be imitated with any real success in English, it sealed its own fate as a beloved visitant to the hearts of the people. Pope and his coterie closed the door on lyrical poets like Thomas Campion, and in their hearts they, like Voltaire, rather despised Shakespeare for his vulgarisms.

The truth that poetry was primarily written to be sung is forgotten, and even in France the chant of the Alexandrine, which both Rachel and Sarah Bernhardt restored, was lost in a monotonous recitation. For myself, I tried to get to the root of the matter by reading Thomas Campion—Charles

Scribner's Sons print a good edition of his songs, masks, etc., edited by A. H. Bullen—as an antidote to Walt Whitman. In fact, my acquaintance with the Poet of Camden convinced me that his use of what is to-day called *vers libre* resembled somewhat Carlyle's Teutonic contortions of style. It was impossible to get from the "Good Gray Poet" the reasons of his method. I gathered that he looked on rhythm as sometimes a walk, a quick-step, a saunter, a hop-and-skip, a hurried dash, or a slow march; it seemed to depend with him on the action of the heart, the acceleration of the pulse, or the movement of the thought.

But no one who knows the best in Walt Whitman's poems can fail to perceive that there were times when he understood thoroughly that poetry, expressed poetically, must be musical. It is a great pity that some of our newer poets do not understand this. In their revolt from the outworn academic rules, they have gone the length of the most advanced Cubists, and do not realize that no amount of splendid visualization compensates for a lack of knowledge of the art of making melodies. It is unfortunate, too, that the imitators of Amy Lowell, many of whom have neither her feeling for colour, her great power of concentration, nor her naturally good ear, should imagine that *vers libre* means the throwing together of words in chaos. Even Strauss's "Electra" is founded on carefully considered rules; his discords are not accidents.

It seems to me that the study of Sidney Lanier's "Science of English Verse" would suppress the art of expression, even in a genius. By the time he learned how to write verse he would be too old to write verse at all! There are less intricate books. I learned from the theories and the odes of Coventry Patmore and the "Observations in the Art of English Poesy" of Thomas Campion and his practice that the best *vers libre* has freedom, unexpectedness, lyrical lightness, and an apparently unstudied charm, because the poet had striven, not to sing as a bird sings, without art, but to sing in a civilized world as a great tenor in the opera sings, because he had acquired his method of almost perfect expression through science and art. And, if one wants an example of the intangible "something," expressed artistically, why not take Benet's "Immoral Ballad"? A little thing, sir; but a poet's own and so, incapable of being analyzed by any rules known to the pundits. But it is not *vers libre*. If it were, its intangible appeal would not exist.

Nearly every versifier who disregards those models of form in verse which include rime, or whose cadences are informal, is set down as an imitator of Walt Whitman. When I was young, Walt Whitman seemed to have been established as a strange, erratic, and godless person, whose indecencies were his principal stock in trade. Emerson's practical repudiation of him had had its effect, and the very respectable—that is, gentlemen of the class of the vestrymen of Grace Church in New York of his time—looked on him with horror. He had, it seems, attacked established religion when he made his onslaught in the Brooklyn *Eagle* on that eminently important body.

The shock of the arrival of Walt Whitman had been broken by the time that I had begun to read poetry wherever I found it; and I accepted the curious mixture of prose and poetry in Walt Whitman just as I accepted the musical Wagner. At that time we had not yet learned to know that Wagner's music was melodious; we had not yet discovered that "Lohengrin," for instance, was woven of many melodies, for they were not detached and made into arias. What could be expected of young persons brought up on "The Bohemian Girl" and "Maritana"?

And yet we soon found out without any help from the critics that Walt Whitman was essentially a poet, and we suspected that his roughness had been deliberately adopted as the best possible form in which to clothe ideas which were not conventional, and to attract attention. Most of the young at that time thought that he had as much right to do this as Browning had to be wilfully inarticulate. The critics did not concern us much. There was always a little coterie of students at the University of Pennsylvania or at Jefferson College, or young men under the influence of Mr. Edward Roth or Mr. Henry Peterson. Among these was a brilliant Mexican, David Cerna; Charles Arthur Henry, who died young; Daniel Dawson, whose "Seeker in the Marshes" ought still to live. He was a devout Whitmanite. Much younger was Harrison Morris, whose opinions, carrying great weight, occasionally floated to us. As I have said, Whitman neither startled nor shocked us nor did he cause us to imitate him. At this time, I was deep in Heinrich Heine, whose prose was not easy to read, but whose lyrics, with a very slight help from the dictionary, were entrancing! I could never understand, being enraptured with Heine's lyrics at that time, why Whitman should have chosen such a poor medium for lyrical expression or such a rude utterance for some noble ideas. That he chose at times to put into speech sensual dreams or passing shadows of evil thoughts astonished us no more than the existence of the photographic reproductions, then the fashion, of the gargoyles from the Cathedral of Notre Dame, or the strange and very improper representations of the Seven Deadly Sins which were sometimes carved on the backs and the undersides of the stalls in old cathedrals. We Philadelphians thought that it was not a gentlemanly performance. There were persons who wallowed in pools of de-civilization, and, though they might whisper of their mental wallowings in intimate circles, there was no point whatever in putting them into print. But the great passages—there are very many—and the noble complete poems—there are a few—of Whitman were chosen and recited and enjoyed.

Besides, Whitman lived just across the Delaware River, and one could meet him almost at any time in a street car or lounging about his haunts in Camden.

As he was part of our everyday life he did not for us represent anything essentially new. When Swinburne and Rossetti and the Preraphaelites, however, came into our possession, it was quite another thing! There was no Whitman movement among our young. There was a marked, but not concentrated, reflection of the Preraphaelites.

Swinburne's music took us by storm! It did not mean that a young man had a depraved mind because he spouted "Faustine" or quoted verse after verse of the roses and raptures of Swinburne. It simply meant that a breath of rich, sensuous odours from an exotic island had swept across the conventional lamp-posts and well-trimmed gardens of his life. I wonder if any young man feels to-day, in reading Masefield's poems, or Walter de la Mare's, or Seeger's, or Amy Lowell's, or Robert Frost's, or even Alfred Noyes's, the thrill that stirred us when we heard the choruses in "Atalanta in Calydon" or Rossetti's "Blessed Damozel"? And there was William Morris and "The Earthly Paradise!"

The first appearance of Kipling's poems recalled the old thrills of "new" poets, but of late, though the prospects of poetry are beginning to revive, no very modern poet seems to have become a part of the daily lives of the young, who declare that the world is changed, and that the Old hold no torches for them by which they can discover what they really want! The more things change, the more they remain the same! And the young woman who read Swinburne surreptitiously and smoked a cigarette in private now reads Havelock Ellis on summer porches, and puffs at a cigarette in public whenever she feels like it. She is really no more advanced than the girl of the period of the eighties, and not any more astonishing. It's the same old girl! And the young men who discovered Swinburne and Rossetti, and who were rather bored by the thinness of their aftermath, the æsthetic poets, really got more colour and amazement and delight out of the flashing of the meteors than the youth of to-day seem to get. It was the fashion then to be blasé and cynical and bored with life; but nobody was really bored because there were too many amusing and delightful things in the world—as there are now.

Joaquin Miller, with his gorgeous parrots and burning Southern lights and his intensities and his simulated passion, did not last long. In England he was looked on as a typical American poet, more decent than Walt Whitman, less vulgar, but with the charm Whitman had for the English—that no Englishman could ever be like him! In England they wanted the Americans raw and fresh and with a savage flavour about them.

I read the poems of Richard Watson Gilder, of Edith Thomas, of Robert Underwood Johnson—whose "Italian Rhapsody" and "The Winter Hour" can never be forgotten—and certain verses of Edmund Clarence Stedman. But *les jeunes* prefer the new verse makers. There is even a kind of cult for the

Imagists. A spokesman for the Imagists tells us briefly that "free verse" is a term that may be attached to all that increasing amount of writing whose cadence is more marked, more definite, and closer knit than that of prose, but which is not so violently or so obviously accented as the so-called "regular verse." Richard Aldington's "Childhood" is a very typical example of *vers libre*. It is also an Imagist poem. It will be remarked that it is so free that there is no cadence that any musician could find. It is a pretty little joyful trifle!

There was nothing to see,
Nothing to do,
Nothing to play with,
Except that in an empty room upstairs
There was a large tin box
Containing reproductions of the Magna Charta,
Of the Declaration of Independence,
And of a letter from Raleigh after the Armada;
There were also several packets of stamps,
Yellow and blue Guatemala parrots,
Blue stags and red baboons and birds from Sarawak,
Indians and Men-of-war
From the United States,
And the green and red portraits
Of King Francobollo
Of Italy.

I don't believe in God
I do believe in avenging gods
Who plague us for sins we never sinned
But who avenge us.
That's why I'll never have a child,
Never shut up in a chrysalis in a match-box
For the moth to spoil and crush its bright colours,
Beating its wings against the dingy prison-wall.

Alfred Kreymborg is also very free, and only sometimes musical, but he hammers in his images with a vengeance. But of all the new Americans, Vachel Lindsay's jolly fantasies, with a slightly heard banjo accompaniment, are the most fascinating and least tiresome of all the New.

When one has wallowed for a time with the Imagists and carefully examined the *vers librists*, with the aid of a catalogue and explanations, one turns to the "Collected Poems" of Walter de la Mare. Come, now! Listen to this:

When slim Sophia mounts her horse
And paces down the avenue,
It seems an inward melody
She paces to.

Each narrow hoof is lifted high
Beneath the dark enclustering pines,
A silver ray within his bit
And bridle shines.

His eye burns deep, his tail is arched,
And streams upon the shadowy air,
The daylight sleeks his jetty flanks,
His mistress' hair.

Her habit flows in darkness down,
Upon the stirrup rests her foot,
Her brow is lifted, as if earth
She heeded not.

'Tis silent in the avenue,
The sombre pines are mute of song,
The blue is dark, there moves no breeze
The boughs among.

When slim Sophia mounts her horse
And paces down the avenue,
It seems an inward melody
She paces to.

It is difficult for the simple minded to understand why Walter de la Mare, who is a singer with something to sing about, cannot be classed as an Imagist. He uses the language of common speech and tries always to say exactly what he means; he suits his mood to his rhythm, and his cadences to his ideas; he believes passionately in the artistic value of modern life; but he does not seem to see why he should not write about an old-fashioned aëroplane of the year 1914, if he can make it the centre of something interesting.

The professional Imagist tries to produce poetry that is hard and clear and never blurred or indefinite, and he holds that concentration is the very essence of poetry. The Imagist fights for "free verse" as for the principle of liberty. But why does he fight? If "free verse" is musical, if it expresses a mood or an emotion or a thought in terms that appeal to the mind or the heart or the imagination, why should it be necessary to fight for it? It may suit certain verse makers to make men of straw in order "to fight" for them; but all the world loves a poet, if the poet once touches its heart. "The Toys" of Coventry Patmore is a good example of what "free verse" ought to be. But it is not free because it is lawless; its freedom is the freedom of all true art which does not ignore, which obediently accepts, certain laws that govern the expression of the beautiful. Mr. Richard Aldington's "Daisy" is certainly a less appealing poem than that one in which Swinburne sings of the lady who forgot his kisses, and he forgot her name!

José de Herédia, in "Les Trophées," is both an Imagist and a Symbolist. He has the inspiration and the science of the Sibyl without her contortions. It is unfortunate that the truculent attitude of the professional makers of "free verse" should have arrayed a small and angry group against them; and this group will have none of Robert Frost, who is certainly a poet and a poet of great courage and originality. There are others, however, who may not be imitators of Robert Frost, but who seem as if they were. Tennyson's "Owl," which is looked on to-day as an example of Victorian idiocy, is really better than Mr. T. S. Eliot's "Cousin Nancy":

Miss Nancy Ellicott
Strode across the hills and broke them,
Rode across the hills and broke them—
The barren New England hills—
Riding to hounds
Over the cow-pasture.

Miss Nancy Ellicott smoked
And danced all the modern dances;
And her aunts were not quite sure how they felt about it,
But they knew that it was modern.

Upon the glazen shelves kept watch
Matthew and Waldo, guardians of the faith,
The army of unalterable law.

The Imagist does not believe in ornament, and this glimpse of character might be uttered in one sentence. Perhaps, however, a tendency to ornamentation might have made the poem at least decorative. After all, when one has emerged from the rarefied atmosphere of the Imagist, the Symbolist, and the *vers librist*, one swims into the splendours of Francis Thompson as one might take refuge from a wooden farmhouse unprotected by trees, in a Gothic spire, a Byzantine altar-piece, or a series of Moorish arabesques. It is a frightful descent from the heaven of Crashaw and the places of the

Seraphim in "The Hound of Heaven," by Francis Thompson, to Richard Aldington.

Each lover of poetry has his favourite poem and his favourite poet, and it has always seemed to me that one of the hardest tasks of the critic is to decide on the position of a poet among poets, or of a poet in relation to life. For myself, to speak modestly, I cannot see how I could condemn the taste of the man who thinks that Browning and Swinburne and Tennyson, and, in fact, nearly all the modern English poets, deserve to be classed indiscriminately together as "inspiring." And I cannot even scorn the man who declares that Tennyson is *demodé* because his heroines are in crinoline and conventional, and his mediæval knights cut out of pasteboard.

By comparison with the original of the "Idylls of the King" this statement seems to be true. Sir Thomas Malory's knights and ladies—by modern standards they would hardly be called "ladies"—do not bear the test of even the most elemental demands of modern taste. They are as different as the characters in Saxo Grammaticus's "Hamblet" are from those in Shakespeare's "Hamlet." But I may enjoy the smoothness of the "Idylls of the King," their bursts of exquisite lyricism, their cadences, and their impossibilities, and at the same time read Sir Thomas Malory with delight. When I hear raptures over Browning and Swinburne, when people grow dithyrambic over John Masefield and Alfred Kreymborg and others new—*chacun à son goût*—I feel that by comparison with Francis Thompson, these poets are not rich. They are poor because they seem to leave out God; that is, the God of the Christians.

Swinburne could never be a real pagan, because he could not escape the shadow of the Crucifixion. Theocritus was a real pagan because he knew neither the sorrow of the Crucifixion nor the joy of the Resurrection. Keats was a lover of Greece, was ardent, inexpressibly beautiful, sensuously charming; but Keats could no more be a real Greek than Shakespeare, in "Julius Cæsar," could be a real Roman. Nor could Tennyson, nor Browning, nor William Morris, nor the Preraphaelites be really out of their time, for they could not understand the essentially religious qualities of the times into which they tried to project themselves.

If you compare the "Idylls" of Tennyson with those idylls of Theocritus he imitated, you easily see that his pictures are not even bad copies of the originals; they are not even paraphrases—to turn again from painting to literature. They are fine in themselves, and the critics of the future, more reasonable than ours and less reactionary, will give them their true place. As for Browning, it is only necessary to read the Italian writers of the Renascence, to find how very modern he is in his poems that touch on that period. He is always modern. With all his efforts he cannot understand that mixture of paganism and Catholicism which made the Renascence possible. He seems to assume that the Catholic Church in the time of the Renascence produced men in whom paganism struggled with Christianity. The fact is that paganism had melted into Christianity and Christianity had given it a new light and a new form.

It was not difficult for an artist of the Renascence to look on a statuette of Leda and the Swan or Danaë and the Descent of Jupiter as a shower of gold, as prefiguring the Incarnation. There was nothing blasphemous in this pagan symbolism of a pagan prophecy of the birth of a God from a virgin. It does not follow that Browning is not powerfully beautiful and essentially poetical, even when he reads modern meanings impossibly into the life of older days. Nevertheless, he is unsatisfactory, as almost all modern poets, when they interpret the past, are unsatisfactory. A great poet may look into his heart and write, but with Tennyson, with Browning, with Swinburne, one feels that very often they mistake the beating of their own hearts for the sound of the pulsations of the hearts of others.

Similarly, modern Christians who claim to be orthodox are sometimes shocked when they are told that Saint Peter, for example, did not believe that a man might not be both circumcised and baptized. According to a common belief, the two could not exist together among the converted Jews. And the modern man of letters seems to think that paganism and Christianity were at odds at all points. A deeper knowledge of the manifestations of religion, before the Reformation, would dissipate an illusion which spoils so much fine modern poetry.

Another point, in applying my canons of criticism to poets whom I love in spite of this defect, is that I find that they have no desire to be united with God—you may call him Jehovah, Jove, or Lord, to quote Pope. They are, as a rule, without mysticism and constantly without that ecstasy which makes Southwell, Crashaw, and the greatest of all the mystical poets writing in English, Francis Thompson, so satisfactory.

Wordsworth may have been transcendental, as Emerson certainly was, but in different ways they made their search for the Absolute, and the search, especially in Wordsworth's case, was fervent. Neither had the splendours, the ecstasies of that love that casteth out fear, the almost fierce and violent fervour of desire, reflected from the Apocalypse of Saint John and the poems of Saint Teresa and of Saint John of the Cross, which we find in Francis Thompson. In this respect, all modern poets pale before him. He sees life as a glory as Baudelaire saw it as a corpse. After a reading of "The Hound of Heaven," with its glorious colour, its glow, its flame, all other modern poets seem to me to be a pale mauve by comparison to its flaming gold and crimson.

To many of my friends who love modern poets each in his degree, this seems unreasonable and even incomprehensible; but to me it is very real; and all literature which assumes to treat our lives as if Christianity did not exist lacks that satisfactory quality which one finds in Dante, in Calderon, in Sir Thomas More, and in Shakespeare. It is possible that the prevalence of doubt in modern poetry is the cause of its lack of gaiety. There is a modern belief that gaiety went out of fashion when Pan died or disappeared into hidden haunts. This is not true. The Greeks were gay at times and joyous at times, but if their philosophers represent them, joyousness and gaiety were not essential points of their lives.

The highest cultivation of its time could not save Athens from despondency and destruction, and when the leaders in the city of Rome came to believe so little in life that only the proletariat had children, it was evident that their very tolerant system of adopting any god that pleased them did not add to the joy of life. The poet, then, who misunderstands the paganism of the Greeks, who does not desire to be united to an absolute Perfection, who is sad by profession, cannot be, according to my canons, a true poet. I speak, not as a critic, but as a man who loves only the poetry that appeals to him.

CHAPTER III

Certain Novelists

My friendship with Thackeray and Dickens was an evolution rather than a discovery. Once having read "Vanity Fair" or "Nicholas Nickleby," the book became not so much a book but a state of mind—and, as is sometimes felt about a friend—it is hard to remember a time when we did not know him!

Mark Twain was a discovery. "The Jumping Frog of Calavaras" and that chuckling scene in "Innocents Abroad," where the unhappy Italian guide introduces Christopher Columbus to the American travellers, were joys indeed. These were more delightful and satisfying than the kind of humour that preceded them—they seemed better than the whimsicalities of Artemus Ward, and not to be compared to the laboured humour of Mrs. Partington. But, leaving out these amusing passages, my pleasure in the works of Mark Twain faded more and more as I came to the age of reason, which is somewhat over twenty-five. It was hard to laugh at Mark after a time. Compared to him, the "Pickwick Papers" had an infinite variety. There were other things in Dickens which were finer than anything in "Pickwick," but the humour of Pickwick had a softness about it, a human interest, a lack of coarseness, which placed it immeasurably above that of Mark Twain.

The greatest failure of Dickens was "A Tale of Two Cities." And the greatest failure of Mark Twain is his "Joan of Arc." But Dickens redeemed himself in a hundred ways, while Mark Twain sank deeper and deeper into coarseness and pessimism. As Mark Twain is by all odds apparently the national American author, it is heresy to say this; and I know persons who have assumed an air of coldness as long as they could in my presence, because I declined to look on "Joan of Arc" as a masterpiece.

It shows some faults of Mark Twain's philosophy of life, it suggests his narrow and materialistic point of view, and makes plain his lack of knowledge of the perspectives of history. It is all the worse for an appearance of tenderness. Mark Twain was neither mystical nor spiritual. That does not mean that he was not a good husband and father, a kind friend and a man very loyal to all his engagements. There are many other authors who had not all these qualities, but who would have more easily understood the character of Joan than did Mark Twain.

Dickens's failure in "A Tale of Two Cities" was from very different causes. It was not through a failure of tenderness, a lack of an understanding of the real pathos of life, or through the want of a spirituality without which no great work can be effective. It was because Dickens relied very largely on Carlyle for the foundation of his study of the historical atmosphere of that novel—the best, from the point of view of style, except "Barnaby Rudge," that he ever wrote, probably due to the fact that, treading as he did on ground that was new to him, he had to guide his steps very carefully. The novel is nevertheless a failure because it is untrue; it concerns itself with a France that never existed seen through as artificial a medium as the mauve tints through which certain artists see their figures and landscapes. It was not with Dickens a case of defect in vision, but a lack of knowledge. It was not lack of perception or the absence of a great power of feeling. It was pure ignorance. He was without that training which would have enabled him to go intelligently to the sources of French history.

In Mark Twain's case it was not a lack of the power to reach the sources; it was an inability to understand the character of the woman whom he reverenced, so far as he could feel reverence, and an invincible ignorance of the character of her time. Mark Twain was modern; but modern in the vulgarest way. I know that "Huckleberry Finn" and the other young Americans—whom our youth are expected to like, if not to imitate—are looked on as sacred by the guardians of those libraries who recommend typical books to eager juvenile readers. But let that pass for the moment. To take a case in point, there is hardly any man or woman of refinement who will hold a brief in defense of the vulgarity of "A Connecticut Yankee at the Court of King Arthur."

It may be said that the average reader of Mark Twain's books—that is, the average American reader—for Mark Twain is read the world over—cares nothing for his philosophy of life. The average American reads Mark Twain only to be amused, or to recall the adventures of a time not far away when we were less sophisticated. Still, whether my compatriots are in the habit of looking into books for a philosophy or not, or of considering the faiths or unfaiths of the writer in hand, it does not follow that it is to their credit if they neglect an analysis which cultivated readers in other countries seldom omit.

If I thought that any words of mine would deprive anybody of the gaiety which Mark Twain has added to life, I should not write these words; but as this little volume is a book of impressions, and sincere impressions, I may be frank in the full understanding that the average American reader will not take seriously what I say of Mark Twain, since he has become an integral part of American literature. There may perhaps come a time when his works will be sold in sets, carefully arranged on all self-respecting bookshelves, pointed to with pride as a proof of culture, and never read. They will perhaps one day be the Rogers's statuettes of literature. But that day is evidently far off. I do not think that any jester of the older day—the day of Touchstone or of Rigoletto, with a rooted sorrow in his heart, could have been more pessimistic and more hopeless than Mark Twain. To change the words of Autolycus—"For the life to come, I jest out the thought of it!"

"You who admire Don Quixote," said an infuriated Mark Twainite, "should not talk of coarseness. There are pages in that romance of Cervantes which I would not allow my son or daughter to read."

One should give both sides of an argument, and I give this other side to show what may be said against my views. But the coarseness of Cervantes is, after all, a healthy coarseness. Modern ideas of purity were not his. Ignorance in those days—the days of Cervantes—did not mean innocence. Even the fathers of the Church were quite willing to admit that the roots of water lilies were in the mud, and there was no conspiracy to conceal the existence of the mud. Mark Twain's coarseness, however, is more than that of Cervantes or Shakespeare. Neither Cervantes nor Shakespeare is ever irreverent.

To them, even the ordinary things of life have a certain sacerdotal quality; but Mark Twain abhorred the sacerdotal quality as nature abhors a vacuum. To say that he has affected the American spirit or the American heart would be to go too far—for Americans are irreverent only on the surface. It seems to me that they are the most reverent people in the world toward those essential qualities which make up the spiritual parts of life. Curiously enough, however, Mark Twain is just at present the one author to whom all Europe and all outlanders point as the great typical American writer!

That a delightful kind of American humour may exist without exaggeration, or the necessity of debasing the moral currency, many joyous books in our literature show. There are a few, of course, that are joyous without self-consciousness; but for real joyousness and charm and innocent gaiety, united to a knowledge of the psychology of the American youth, none so far has equalled Booth Tarkington's "Penrod," or, what is better, "Seventeen."

Now nobody has yet done anything so delightful, so mirth provoking, so pathetic, in a way, as "Seventeen." In my youth I was deprived of the knowledge of this book, for when I swam into the tide of literature, Booth Tarkington was in that world from which Wordsworth's boy came, bringing rainbows, which moved to all the music of the spheres. It was during the late war that "Seventeen" was cast on the coasts of Denmark, at a time when American books scarcely reached those coasts at all. St. Julian, the patron of merry travellers, must have guided it through the maze and labyrinths of bombs and submarines in the North Sea. It arrived just when the world seemed altogether upside down; when death was the only real thing in life, and pain as much a part of the daily routine as the sunshine, and when joy seemed to have been inexplicably crushed from the earth, because sorrow was ever so recurrent that it could not be forgotten for a moment. Then "Seventeen" arrived.

Booth Tarkington may have his ups and downs in future, as he has had in the past. "The Gentleman from Indiana" seemed to me to be almost one of the most tiresome books ever invented, while "Monsieur Beaucaire" was one of the most fascinating, charming. You can hardly find a better novel of American life than "The Turmoil," unless it is Judge Grant's "Unleavened Bread."

But the best novels of American life seem to be written in order to be forgotten. Who reads "The Breadwinners" now? Or who, except the professional "teacher" of literature, recalls "Prue and I"? Or that succession of Mrs. Harriet Beecher Stowe's novels, almost unequalled as pictures of a section of our life, each of which better expresses her talent than "Uncle Tom's Cabin"? The English and the French have longer memories. Mrs. Oliphant's "Chronicles of Carlingford"—some of us remember "Miss Majoribanks" or "Phœbe Junior"—finds a slowly decreasing circle of readers. And while "Sapho" is almost forgotten, "Les Rois en Exilé" and "Jack" are still parts of current French literature. But "Unleavened Bread" or "The Damnation of Theron Ware" or "Elsie Venner" or the "Saxe Holm's Stories" are so much of the past as to be unread.

To the credit of the gentle reader, Miss Alcott's stories perennially bloom. And, for some strange reason, the weird "Elsie Dinsmore" series is found under the popular Christmas tree, while nobody gives the Rollo books to anybody. Why? One may begin to believe that that degeneracy which the prevalence of jazz, lip-sticks, and ballet costumes adapted to the subway is supposed to indicate, is a real menace when one discovers that "Penrod" or "Seventeen" has ceased to be read!

We may read Mark Twain and wallow in vulgarity, but it is my belief that Sodom and Gomorrah would have escaped their fate, if a Carnegie of that time had made it possible to keep books like "Penrod" and "Seventeen" in general circulation!

It was once said of Anthony Trollope that as long as English men and women of the upper and middle classes continued to exist, he might go on writing novels with ever-increasing zest. And the same thing might be said of Booth Tarkington in relation to his unique chronicles of youth—that is, the youth of the Middle West, with a universal Soul. His types are American, but there are Americas and Americas. Usage permits us to use a term for our part of the continent to which our Canadian and South and Central Americans and Mexicans might reasonably object; but while the young Americans of Booth Tarkington are typically American, they personally could belong only to the Middle West. The hero of "Seventeen" would not be the same boy if he had been born in Philadelphia or New York or Boston. Circumstances would have made him different. The consciousness of class distinction would have made him old before his time; and though he might be just as amusing—he would not have been amusing quite in the same way.

And this is one of the fine qualities of Mr. Tarkington's imaginative synthesis. He is individual and of his own soil; he knows very well that it is unnecessary to exaggerate or even to invent; he has only to perceive with those rare gifts of perception which he possesses. It all seems so easy until you try to do it yourself!

The state of mind of Penrod, when he is being prepared for the pageant of the "Table Round," is inexpressibly amusing to the adult reader; but no child can look on it as entirely amusing, because every child has suffered more or less, as Penrod suffered, from the unexplainable hardness of heart and dullness of mind of older people. Something or other prevents the most persecuted boy from admitting that his parents are bad parents because they force impositions which tear all the fibres of his soul and make him helpless before a jeering world. When Penrod has gone through horrors, which are nameless because they seem to be so unreasonable, he murmurs aloud, "*Well, hasn't this been a day!*" Because of the humour in "Penrod" there is a pathos as true and real as those parts in the "Pickwick Papers" where fortunately Dickens is pathetic in a real sense because he did not strive for pathos. Everybody admits now that Dickens becomes almost repellent when he wilfully tries to be pathetic.

One could pick out of "Seventeen" a score of delightful situations which seem to ripple from the pen of Booth Tarkington, one of the best being the scene between the hero and his mother when that *esprit terrible*, his sister, seems to stand between him and the lady of his thoughts. And "Penrod" is full of them. The description of that young gallant's entrance into society is of Mr. Tarkington's best. Penrod is expected to find, according to the rules of dancing academies, a partner for the cotillion. It is his duty to call on the only young lady unengaged, who was Miss Rennsdale, aged eight. Penrod, carefully tutored, makes his call.

A decorous maid conducted the long-belated applicant to her where she sat upon a sofa beside a nursery governess. The decorous maid announced him composedly as he made his entrance.

"Mr. Penrod Schofield!"

Miss Rennsdale suddenly burst into loud sobs.

"Oh!" she wailed. "I just knew it would be him!"

The decorous maid's composure vanished at once—likewise her decorum. She clapped her hand over her mouth and fled, uttering sounds. The governess, however, set herself to comfort her heartbroken charge, and presently succeeded in restoring Miss Rennsdale to a semblance of that poise with which a lady receives callers and accepts invitations to dance cotillons. But she continued to sob at intervals.

Feeling himself at perhaps a disadvantage, Penrod made offer of his hand for the morrow with a little embarrassment. Following the form prescribed by Professor Bartet, he advanced several paces toward the stricken lady and bowed formally.

"I hope," he said by rote, "you're well, and your parents also in good health. May I have the pleasure of dancing the cotillon as your partner t'-morrow afternoon?"

The wet eyes of Miss Rennsdale searched his countenance without pleasure, and a shudder wrung her small shoulders; but the governess whispered to her instructively, and she made a great effort.

"I thu-thank you fu-for your polite invu-invu-invutation; and I ac——" Thus far she progressed when emotion overcame her again. She beat frantically upon the sofa with fists and heels. "Oh, I did want it to be Georgie Bassett!"

"No, no, no!" said the governess, and whispered urgently, whereupon Miss Rennsdale was able to complete her acceptance.

"And I ac-accept wu-with pu-pleasure!" she moaned, and immediately, uttering a loud yell, flung herself face downward upon the sofa, clutching her governess convulsively.

Somewhat disconcerted, Penrod bowed again.

"I thank you for your polite acceptance," he murmured hurriedly; "and I trust—I trust—I forget. Oh, yes—I trust we shall have a most enjoyable occasion. Pray present my compliments to your parents; and I must now wish you a very good afternoon."

Concluding these courtly demonstrations with another bow he withdrew in fair order, though thrown into partial confusion in the hall by a final wail from his crushed hostess:

"Oh! Why couldn't it be anybody but him!"

Dickens would not have done the scene quite this way; he could not have so conceived it, and he might have overdone it, but Booth Tarkington gets it just right. He has created boy characters which will live because they are alive. One of the most detestable books, after Mark Twain's "Yankee at the Court of King Arthur," is Dickens's "Child's History of England." The two books have various gross faults in common and these faults are due to colossal ignorance. Mr. Gilbert Chesterton says that one of Dickens's is due to the application of a plain rule of right and wrong to all circumstances to which it was applied. It is not that they wrongly enforce the fixed principle that life should be saved; it is that they take a fire-engine to a shipwreck and a life-boat to a house on fire. The business of a good man in Dickens's time was to bring justice up to date. The business of a good man in Dunstan's time was to toil to ensure the survival of any justice at all.

It seems to me that if all the works of Dickens were lost we might do very well with the "Pickwick Papers" and "Nicholas Nickleby." To these, one is tempted to add "Our Mutual Friend."

When I was young enough to assist at meetings of Literary Societies, where papers on Dickens were read, I was invariably informed that "Charles Dickens could not paint a lady or a gentleman." There was no reason given for this censure. It was presumed that the authors of the papers meant an English lady or gentleman. Nobody, to my knowledge, ever defined what an English gentleman or lady was. When one considers that for a long period an English gentleman's status was determined by the fact that he owned land, had not even a remote connection with "trade" or that he was instructed at Eton or Harrow, in Oxford or Cambridge, the more modern definition would have been very different from what the English of the olden time would have called a gentleman. Even now, when a levelling education has rather blurred the surface marks of class in England, it might be difficult for an American to define what was meant by this criticism of Dickens. It seems to me that no one could define exactly what was meant. The convention that makes the poet in Pennsylvania write as if the banks of the Wissahickon were peopled by thrushes, or orchestrated by the mavis, or the soaring lark, causes him often to borrow words from the English vocabulary of England without analyzing their exact meaning. There can be no doubt that Don Quixote was a gentleman but not exactly in the English conventional sense. And, if he was a gentleman, why are not Mr. Pickwick and Sam Weller gentlemen? An interesting thesis might be written on the application of Cardinal Newman's definition of a gentleman to both Mr. Pickwick and Sam Weller. Why not?

There is a truth about the English people, at least the lower classes, which Mr. Chesterton in his illuminating "Appreciations and Criticisms of the Works of Charles Dickens"—one of his best books—brings out, though he does not accentuate it sufficiently: this is that the lower classes of the English are both witty and humorous. Witty because they are satirical and humorous because they are ironical. Sam Weller represents a type—a common type—more exactly than Samuel Lover's "Handy Andy" or any of Charles Lever's Irish characters. When one examines the foundation for the assertion that Dickens could not draw a lady or a gentleman, one discovers that his ladies and gentlemen, in the English sense, are deadly dull. It is very probable that all conventional ladies and gentlemen bored Dickens, who never ceased to be a cockney, though he became the most sublimated of that class. Doctor Johnson was a cockney, too, but, though it may seem paradoxical to say it, not so greatly impressed by class distinctions as Dickens was.

Dickens had the art of making insupportable bores most interesting. This was an art in which the delicate Miss Austen excelled, too; but Dickens's methods compared to hers are like those of a scene painter when compared to those of an etcher in colours. There are times when Dickens is consciously "common," and then he is almost unbearable; but this objection cannot be made to the "Pickwick Papers." This book is inartistic; it is made up of unrelated parts; the characters do not grow; they change. But all this makes no difference. They are spontaneous. You feel that for once Dickens is doing the thing he likes to do—and all the world loves a lover who loves his work.

There are doubtless some people still living who can tolerate the romantic quality in "Nicholas Nickleby." There are no really romantic qualities in the "Pickwick Papers"—thank heaven!—no stick of a hero, no weeping willow of a heroine. The heroic sticks of Dickens never bloom suddenly as the branch in "Tannhäuser" bloomed. Even Dickens can work no miracle there.

It increases our admiration of him to examine the works of those gentlemen who are set down in the textbooks of literature as his predecessors. Some of these learned authors mention Sterne's "Tristram Shandy," a very dull and tiresome narrative; and "Tom Jones," very tiresome, too, in spite of its fidelity to certain phases of eighteenth-century life. And later, Pierce Egan's "Tom and Jerry." I was brought up to consider the renown of the two Pierce Egans with reverence and permitted to read "Tom and Jerry; or The Adventures of Corinthian Bob" as part of the family pedigree, but it requires the meticulous analysis of a German research-worker to find any real resemblance between the artificial dissipations of "Tom and Jerry" and the adventures of the peerless Pickwick.

If the elder Pierce Egan had the power of influencing disciples, he ought to have induced his son to produce something better than "The Poor Boy; or, The Betrayed Baffled," "The Fair Lilias," and others too numerous to mention.

The voracious reader of Dickens, as he grows older, perhaps becomes a student of Dickens, and is surprised to find that the development of Dickens is much more marked and easily noted than the development of Thackeray. In fact, Thackeray, like his mild reflector, Du Maurier, sprang into the public light fully equipped and fully armed. Both these men had wide experience and a careful training in form and proportion before they attempted to write seriously. They were educated in art and life and letters. The education of

Dickens, on the other hand, was only begun with "Pickwick," which knew neither method nor proportion; and he who reads "Barnaby Rudge" for the flavour of Dickens finds a new and good perspective and proportion, and even self-restraint. Artistically, it is the best of all Dickens's novels. For that reason it lacks that flavour which we find in the earlier books. I could not get such thorough enjoyment from it as from "Nicholas Nickleby." In it Dickens sacrificed too much to his self-restraint, and there is no moment in it that gives us the joy of the discovery of Mr. and Mrs. Vincent Crummles or of 'Tilda Price.

Anthony Trollope, in his "Autobiography," which ought to be a textbook in all those practical classes of literature that work to turn out self-supporting authors, tells us that the most important part of a novel is the plot. This may be true, but the inefficiency of the plot in the works of Charles Dickens may easily be shown in an attempt to summarize any of them, except "The Mystery of Edwin Drood."

Still, when all is said for Dickens, one cannot even in old age begin to read him over and over again, as one can read Thackeray. But who reads an American book over and over again? Hawthorne never wearies the elect, and one may go back to Henry James, in order to discover whether one thinks that he means the same thing in 1922 one thought he meant in 1912. But who makes it a practice in middle age to read any novel of Mrs. Wharton's or Mrs. Deland's or Mr. Marion Crawford's or Mr. Booth Tarkington's at least once a year? There are thousands of persons who find leisure to love Miss Austen, that hardiest of hardy perennials; and during the war, when life in the daytime became a nightmare, there was a large group of persons who read Trollope from end to end! This is almost incredible; but it is true. And I must confess that if I do not read Miss Austen's novels once every year, preferably cozily in the winter, or "Cranford," or parts of Froissart—whose chronicle takes the bad taste of Mark Twain's "Joan of Arc" from my memory—I feel as if I had had an ill-spent year. It makes me seem as slothful as if I omitted a daily passage from "The Following of Christ" or, at least, a weekly chapter from the Epistles of St. Paul!

George Eliot I had known even before the time I had begun to read. No well-brought-up child could escape "Adam Bede" and the drolleries of Mrs. Poyser. As I grew older, however, "Romola" attracted me most. The heroine is perhaps a little too good for human nature's daily food, but she is a great figure in the picture. I suspect that the artificiality of Kingsley's "Hypatia," which I read at almost the same time, made me admire, if I did not love, Romola, by way of contrast. No youth could ever love Romola as Walter Scott made him love Mary Stuart or Catherine Seton. But as it happened that just at this time I was labouring with Blackstone (Judge Sharswood's Notes), with a volume of scholastic philosophy "on the side"—I think it was

Jourdain's *consommé* of St. Thomas Aquinas in French—Romola was a decided relief, and she seemed truer and more interesting in every way than Hypatia, who was as *papier-maché* as her whole environment is untrue to the history of the time. An historical novel ought not necessarily to be true to history, but it ought to be illuminating and interesting, as "Hypatia" is not and as "Romola" is. So it makes no difference whether George Eliot's reading of Savonarola is correct or not, though it ought to be correct, of course. Then there is Tito, the delicious and treacherous Tito! and the scene in the barber shop! And if you want a good, mouth-filling novel, give me "Middlemarch." Few persons read it now, and probably fewer will read it in the future. It is nevertheless a great monument to the genius of a woman who had such an infinite quality for taking pains, that it almost defeated the end for which she worked.

CHAPTER IV

Letters, Biographies, and Memoirs

Some of us have acquired a state of mind which helps us to believe that whenever a man mentions a book he either condemns or approves of it. In a word, the mere naming a book means a criticism of the book at once. It is true that books are criticisms of life, and that life, if it is not very narrow and limited, is a good criticism of books; but one of the most pleasant qualities of a reader who has lived among books all his life is that he does not attempt always to recommend books to others, or to preach about them. Besides, it is too dangerous to recommend unreservedly or to condemn unreservedly. The teachers of literature have undertaken the recommendation of books for the young; there are schools of critics who spend their time in approving of them for the old; and the "Index" at Rome assumes the difficult task of disapproval and condemnation. That lets me out, I feel.

One of my most cherished books is the "Letters to People in the World," by Saint Francis de Sales. I have known people who have declared that it is entirely exotic and has no meaning whatever for them. For me, it is a book of edification and a guide to life; and the "Letters" of Saint Francis himself, not entirely concerned with spiritual matters or the relations of spiritual matters to life, are to me a constant source of pleasure. I remember reading aloud to a friend the passage in which this charming Bishop writes that, when he slept at his paternal château, he never allowed the peasants on the domain to perform their usual duty, which was to stay up all night and beat the waters of the ponds, or perhaps of the moat, around the castle, so that the seigneur and his friends might sleep peacefully. My friend was very much bored and could not see that it represented a social point of view, which showed that the Saint was much ahead of his time! It did not bring old France back to him; he could not see the old château and the water in the moonlight, or conceive how glad the peasants were to be relieved of their duty. I can read the "Letters" of Saint Francis de Sales over and over again, as I read the "Letters" of Madame de Sévigné or the "Memoirs" of the Duc de Saint Simon.

I think I first made acquaintance of Saint Simon in an English translation by Bayle St. John. If you have an interest in interiors—the interiors of rooms, of gardens, of palaces—you must like Saint Simon. Most people to-day read these "Memoirs" in little "collections"; but I think it is worth while taking the trouble to learn French in order to become an understanding companion of this malicious but very graphic author. To me the Palace of Versailles would be an empty desert without the "Memoirs" of Saint Simon. Else, how could anybody realize a picture of Mademoiselle de la Vallière looking hopelessly out of the window of her little room just before the birth of her child? Or what would the chapel be without a memory of those devout ladies who knelt regularly, holding candles to their faces, at the exercises in Lent, after Louis XIV. had become devout, in order that he might see them?

But because I love to linger in the society of the Duc de Saint Simon and Cardinal de Retz, it does not follow that I mean to introduce modern and ingenuous youth to the society of these gentlemen. Each man has his pet book. I still retain a great affection for a man of my own age who gives on birthdays and great feasts copies of "The Wide, Wide World" and "Queechy" to his grandchildren and their friends! Could you believe that? He dislikes Miss Austen's novels and sneers at Miss Farrar's "Marriage." He has never been able to read Miss Edgeworth's book; and he considers Pepys's "Diary" an immoral book! Now, I find it very hard to exist without at least a weekly peep into Pepys. And, by the way, in a number of the *Atlantic Monthly* not so long ago there is a vivid, pathetic, and excellently written piece of literature. It is "A Portion of the Diurnal of Mrs Eliz^th Pepys" by E. Barrington.

If anybody asks me why I like Pepys, I do not feel obliged to reply. I might incriminate myself. Very often, indeed, by answering a direct question about books, one does incriminate oneself.

However, to return to what I was saying—while I love the "Memoirs of Cardinal de Retz," I adore—to be a little extravagant—the "Letters of Saint Vincent de Paul." The man that does not know the real story of the life of Saint Vincent de Paul knows nothing of the evolution of the brotherhood of man in the seventeenth century. This Frenchman really fought with beasts for the life of children, and was the only real reformer in the France of his time.

Now it is not because Saint Vincent was for a time the preceptor of Cardinal de Retz that I find the Cardinal so delightful! On the contrary! I enjoy the Cardinal, famous coadjutor of his uncle, the Archbishop of Paris, because he is a true type of the polite, the worldly, and the intriguing gentleman of his time. He died a good peaceful death, as all the gay and the gallant did at his time. He earned the deepest affection and respect of Madame de Sévigné, for which any discerning man might have been willing to spend half a lifetime. But even that is beside the point. He lives for me because he gives a picture of the French ruling classes of his time which is shamelessly true. No living man to-day in political office, although he might be as great an intriguer as the Cardinal, would dare to be so interestingly shameless. That is a great charm in itself. And, then, if you read him in French, you discover that he knew how to make literature.

The only wonder in my mind has always been how a man who became so penitent during the last years of his life as Paul de Gondi should not have been forced by his confessor to destroy his book of revelations. But one must remember that the confessors of his period—the period of the founding of the French Academy—had a great respect for mere literature. His father was Philip Emanuel de Gondi, Count de Joigni, General of the Gallies of France, and Knight of the Order of the Holy Ghost; who retired in the year 1640, to live among the Fathers of the Oratory. There he entered into holy orders, and there he died, with the reputation of a mightily pious man, on June 29, 1662, aged eighty-one.

Give me leave, madame [Cardinal de Retz says] to reflect a little here upon the nature of the mind of man. I believe that there was not in the world a man of an uprighter heart than my father, and I may say that he was stampt in the very mold of virtue. Yet my duels and love-intrigues did not hinder the good man from doing all he could to tye to the Church, the soul in the world perhaps the least ecclesiastical. His predilection for his eldest son, and the view of the archbishoprick of Paris for me, were the true causes of his acting thus; though he neither believed it, nor felt it. I dare say that he thought, nay would have sworn, that he was led in all this by no other motive than the spiritual good of my soul, and the fear of the danger to which it might be exposed in another profession. So true it is that nothing is more subject to delusion than piety. All manner of errors creep and hide themselves under that vail. Piety takes for sacred all her imaginations, of what sort soever; but the best intention in the world is not enough to keep it in that respect free from irregularity. In fine, after all that I have related I remained a churchman; but certainly I had not long continued so, if an accident had not happened which I am now to acquaint you with.

This is not at all what is called "edifying," but, from the moral point of view, it shows what Saint Vincent de Paul had to struggle against in the Church of France; and the position of Paul de Gondi in relation to an established church was just as common in contemporary England, where "livings" were matters of barter and sale but where the methods of the clergymen highly placed were neither so intellectual nor so romantic.

It must be admitted that Cardinal de Retz, like a later French prelate, Talleyrand, made no pretense of being fitted for the Church. Talleyrand's only qualification was that he was lame; and, as a younger son, he had to be provided for. But Cardinal de Retz, with all his faults, had a saving grace in spite of many unsaving graces. He did his best to escape the priesthood. He fought his first duel with Bassompierre behind the Convent of the Minims, in the Bois de Vincennes; but it was of no use. His friends stopped the inquiry of the Attorney General, "and so I remained in my cassock notwithstanding my duel." His next duel was with Praslin. He tried his best to give it the utmost publicity, but, he says, "there's no use in opposing one's destiny; nobody took the slightest notice of the scandal."

The elder Dumas has probably had his day, though "Monte Cristo" and "The Three Musketeers" are still read. The newer romance writers are less diffuse, and, not writing *feuilletons*, are not forced to be diffuse. The constant reader of French memoirs of the seventeenth century can hardly help wondering why anybody should read Dumas who could go directly to the sources of his romances.

Speaking of the relation of books to books, it was the "Memoirs" of Madame Campan that took me into the society of Benjamin Franklin. There were legends about him in Philadelphia, where we thought we knew more about this distinguished American than anybody else; but it was through certain passages in the "Memoirs on Marie Antoinette and her Court" that I turned to his autobiography, and then to such letters of his as could be found. That autobiography is one of the gems of American history, though it does not reveal the whole man. If he had been as frank as Cardinal de Retz, his autobiography would have been suppressed; but, then, no Philadelphian could ever be quite frank in his memoirs. It has never been done! Even the seemingly reckless James Huneker understood that thoroughly. But the autobiography of Benjamin Franklin is sufficiently frank. It is of its own time, and it seems to me that it should be read just after one has finished for the second or third time the memoirs of Gouverneur Morris. Everybody feels it his duty to acclaim the charm of the confessions of Benvenuto Cellini, and I have known a young woman who read them reverently in the holy service of culture as a pendant to a textbook on the Renascence, and followed him by Jowett's translation of the "Republic of Plato." She may safely be left to her fate. The diaries of Gouverneur Morris were not in her course of reading, and they seem almost to have been forgotten. I do not recommend them to anybody. There are passages in them which might shock the Prohibitionist, and also those persons who believe in divorce *à la mode de* Madame de Staël.

For me, they are not only constantly amusing, constantly instructive, but they give the best pictures of Parisian interiors of the time before and during the French Revolution. Because I am firmly convinced of this, is it necessary that I should be expected to place them among the Best One Hundred Books? To me they will be always among my best twenty-five books.

In the first place Gouverneur Morris knew well how to serve his country efficiently; and he was too sensible of the debt of that country to France and too sympathetic with the essential genius of the French people not to do his best to serve her, too. The original verses in his memoirs are the worst things in the volumes; but then, everybody has the faults of his virtues, and nearly everybody wrote verses at that time. He was one of the wisest of all our diplomatists. He was broad minded, cultivated, plastic within reasonable limits, and not corroded with a venom of partisan politics. I repeat, with a polite anticipation of contradiction, that no better picture has ever been given of the aristocratic society of the late eighteenth century in Paris.

His gallantries are amusing; yet there is underneath his affectation of the frivolous vice of the time, which might be euphemistically called "exaggerated chivalry, a fundamental morality which one does not find in that class of systematic *roués*" who were astonished at the virtue of the ladies at Newport when the Count de Lauzun and his friends dwelt in that town. There may be dull pages in these memoirs, but if so I have not yet found them.

In "The Diary and Letters" there are many bits of gossip about certain great persons, notably about Talleyrand, who got rid of his mitre as soon as he could, and Madame de Flahaut. It seems to me that Talleyrand and Philippe Égalité were the most fascinating characters of the French Revolution, for the same reason perhaps that moved a small boy who was listening to a particularly dull history of the New Testament to exclaim suddenly, "Oh, skip about the other apostles; read to me about Judas!"

To persons who might censure Gouverneur Morris's frankness one may quote a short passage from Boswell's "Johnson." "To discover such weakness," said Mrs. Thrale to Doctor Johnson, speaking of the autobiography of Sir Robert Sibbald, "exposes a man when he is gone." "Nay," said the pious and great lexicographer, "it is an honest picture of human nature."

This, then, excuses the clever and wise Gouverneur Morris for enlightening us as to the paternity of a son of Madame de Flahaut. Morris, for a time that condoned the amourettes of Benjamin Franklin, was virtuous. Madame de Flahaut, afterward Madame de Souza, gave Morris a hint that he might easily supplant Talleyrand in her affection. "I may, if I please, wean her from all regard toward him, but he is the father of her child, and it would be unjust." In this noble moment Mr. Morris chivalrously forgets the existence of the Count de Flahaut!

In 1789, Mr. Morris continues to write platonic verses to Madame de Flahaut; the Queen's circle at Versailles is worried about the fidelity of the troops; the Count d'Artois holds high revelry in the Orangery; De Launey's head is carried on a pipe in the streets of Paris, and murdered men lie in the gutters. But the fashionable life of Paris is not disturbed. Mr. Morris goes to dinner. He is invited for three o'clock, to the house of Madame la Comtesse de Beauharnais. Toward five o'clock the Countess herself came to announce dinner. Morris is happy in the belief that his hunger will be equal to the delayed feast. For this day, he thinks he will be free from his enemy, indigestion. He is corroborated in his opinion that Madame de Beauharnais is a poetess by a very narrow escape from some rancid butter of which the cook had been very liberal.

But this is froth, and yet indicative of the depth beneath. It seems to me that there is no more interesting and useful book on the French Revolution than this autobiography. It ought to be placed near De Tocqueville's "Ancient Régime" and "Democracy in America."

On December 2, 1800, he believed it to be the general opinion that Mr. Jefferson was considered a demagogue, and that Aaron Burr would be chosen President by the House of Representatives. The gentlemen of the House of Representatives believed that Burr was vigorous, energetic, just, and generous, and that Mr. Jefferson was "afflicted with all the cold-blooded vices, and particularly dangerous from false principles of government which he had imbibed." Virginia would be, of course, against Burr, because, Morris writes,

Virginia can not bear to see any other than a Virginian in the President's chair!

John Adams was President and Thomas Jefferson vice-President, in 1800. It is edifying for us who look on the "demigods" of 1787 with profound reverence, to see them at close range in Gouverneur Morris's pages.

Washington fares well at his hands, Lafayette not nearly so well:

one could not expect the blast of a trumpet from a whistle.

But, then, Morris had had money transactions with the Lafayettes. Morris believed that no man ever existed who controlled himself so well as Washington. Shall we put the "Diary" just after the "Autobiography of Benjamin Franklin," not far from Beveridge's "Marshall" and at least on the same shelf with the perennial Boswell?

I read the confessions of Cardinal de Retz and of Gouverneur Morris many times with a dip now and then, by way of a change, into the Autobiography of Anthony Trollope. This is rather a change from the kickshaws of France to the roast beef of old England. This autobiography never seems to me to be merely a book made to encourage authors to be industrious and hard-working. It is more than that. It is the expression of the life of an unusual man, who did an unusual thing, and who writes about himself so well and so sincerely that he gives us an insight into a phase of English character which none of his novels ever elaborated.

What Trollope did may be done again, but hardly in the American atmosphere, with the restless American nerves and that lack of doggedness which characterizes us. The picture Trollope gives of himself as a member of the English gentry, deprived of all the advantages of his caste except an inborn class feeling, is worth while, and the absence of self-pity is at once brave and pathetic. He knew very well what he wanted, and he secured it by the most honest and direct means. He knew he could get nothing without work, and he worked. His exercise of literature as an avocation did not prevent him from being a good public servant.

As a typical Englishman brought up in the country, he liked to hunt. Hunting is a prerogative of the leisurely and the rich. He obtained leisure at a great sacrifice, and he became fairly rich through the same sacrifice. He tells us of all this with a manliness and lack of sentimentalism which endears this book to me. It is so much the fashion in our day to declare that society is against us when we have to work unremittingly for what we want, that Trollope's honesty is refreshing, and, though most readers will consider the word rather absurd as applied to him—inspiring!

In earlier days every American was brought up with a prejudice against Mrs. Trollope's "Domestic Manners of the Americans," as we were all taught to hate "American Notes," by Dickens. We all softened toward Dickens later, and it would be difficult to read the simply told story of the heroic devotion and courage which Trollope relates of his mother without believing that the recording angel in no way holds her responsible for her rather vulgar book.

How fascinating to the budding author is the record of sales of the books written by Trollope as he ascended the ladder of popularity! How he managed to cajole the publishers in the beginning he does not tell us. They are not so easily managed now. And there is the story of the pious editor who began the serial publication of "Rachel Ray," and although paying Trollope his honorarium, stopped it abruptly because there was a dancing party in the story! In all this the author of "The Warden" and "Barchester Towers" nothing extenuates nor puts down aught in malice. And I must say that for me this autobiography is very good reading. As the sailor once said of a piece of rather solid beef, "There's a great deal of chaw in it."

I pause a moment to reflect on a letter which I have just received from a young college woman who has so far read the manuscript of this book. She writes that it is really not a book so far for professing Christians.

My mother and I had expected of you something more edifying, something that would lead us to the reading of good and elevating books. At college I looked on literature as something apart. Since I have come home to Georgia, I find that it is better for me to submit myself to the direction of our good Baptist clergyman, and have no books on our library shelves that I cannot read aloud to the young. One of your favourites, Madame de Sévigné, shocks me by the cruelty of her description of the death of the famous poisoner, Madame de Brinvilliers. And I do not think that the pages of the Duc de Saint-Simon should be read by young people.

This is an example of what a refined atmosphere may do to a Georgia girl! I have written to her by way of an apology that this is a little volume of impressions and confessions, and that personally I should find life rather duller if I had not the Duc de Saint-Simon at hand. Besides, I do not think that there is a single young person of my acquaintance who would allow me to read any of his pages to him or her!

Most young persons prefer "Main Street" or any other novel that happens to be the vogue. As I have said, I do not agree with Madame de Sévigné when she says, writing of her granddaughter, that bad books ought to be preferred to no books at all. But it would be almost better for the young not to begin to read until they are old, if one is to gauge the value of books by the unfledged taste of youth. Purity, after all, is not ignorance, though a certain amount of ignorance at a certain age is very desirable.

While I write this, I have in mind a little essay of great charm and value by Coventry Patmore on "Modern Ideas of Purity," which goes deeper into the fundamentals of morality than any other modern work on the subject. And, by the way, having read "The Age of Innocence," "Main Street," "Moon Calf," "Miss Lulu Bett," and several other novels, I turn from their lack of gaiety to find a reason why art should not be gloomy, and here it is, from Coventry Patmore's "Cheerfulness in Life and Art."

"Rejoice always: and again I say, Rejoice," says one of the highest authorities; and a poet who is scarcely less infallible in psychological science writes, "A cheerful heart is what the Muses love."

Dante shows Melancholy dismally punished in Purgatory; though his own interior gaiety—of which a word by and by—is so interior, and its outward aspect often so grim, that he is vulgarly considered to have himself been a sinner in this sort. Good art is nothing but a representation of life; and that the good are gay is a commonplace, and one which, strange to say, is as generally disbelieved as it is, when rightly understood, undeniably true. The good and brave heart is always gay in this sense: that, although it may be afflicted and oppressed by its own misfortunes and those of others, it refuses in the darkest moment to consent to despondency; and thus a habit of mind is formed which can discern in most of its own afflictions some cause for grave rejoicing, and can thence infer at least a probability of such cause in cases where it cannot be discerned. Regarding thus cheerfully and hopefully its own sorrows, it is not overtroubled by those of others, however tender and helpful its sympathies may be. It is impossible to weep much for that in others which we should smile at in ourselves; and when we see a soul writhing like a worm under what seems to us a small misfortune, our pity for its misery is much mitigated by contempt for its cowardice.

There may be gaiety and joy in the novels of Harold Bell Wright and Mrs. Gene Stratton-Porter, but it seems to me to be a cheerfulness which is not quite the real thing. It is too sentimental and rather too laboured. These two authors, who, if the value of a writer could really depend on the majority of the votes cast for him, would, with the goldenrod, be our national flowers, seem to work too hard in the pursuit of cheerfulness.

Once I remember asking a scornful Englishman what supported the pleasant town of Stratford-on-Avon. He replied at once, "The Shakespearian industry!" Now the cheerfulness of both Mr. Harold Bell Wright and Mrs. Gene Stratton-Porter, like the cheerfulness of "Pollyanna," seems to be very much of an industry. It is not at all like the joyousness, that delight in life, spontaneous and unconscious, which one finds in the really great authors. Why the modern realist should believe that to be real he must be joyless—in the United States, at least—is perhaps because he feels the public need of protest against the optimistic sentimentalism of the Harold Bell Wrights and the Gene Stratton-Porters. But it would be a serious mistake to assume that neither Mr. Wright nor Mrs. Porter has a gleam of value. It is just as serious a mistake as to assume that the late Mary Jane Holmes and Mrs. E. D. E. N. Southworth had no value. They pleased exactly the same class of people, in their day, which delights in Mr. Wright and Mrs. Porter in ours. They answered to the demand of a public that is moral and religious, that needs to be taken into countries which savoured something of Fairyland, and yet which are framed by reality. However, as long as Mrs. Gene Stratton-Porter and Mr. Harold Bell Wright, and novelists of higher philosophical aspirations, like the author of "The Age of Innocence," and "Blind Mice," and "Zell," and "Main Street," continue to write, there is no danger that the general crowd of American readers will be shocked or corrupted by the "Memoirs" of the Duc de Saint-Simon or of the Comtesse de Boigne. So I feel that I am absolved from the responsibility of misleading any young reader to sup on the horrors of the description of the death of Madame de Brinvilliers as painted by Madame de Sévigné or to revel among the groups of Italians who range through the scenes drawn by Benvenuto Cellini.

While Pepys is always near at hand, I treat his contemporary, Evelyn, with very distant politeness and respect. Now Evelyn should not be treated in that way. He is always so edifying and so very correct, except when he moralizes about the Church of Rome, that he ought to be read nearly every day by the serious as an example of propriety and as a model of the expression of the finest sentiments on morals, philosophy, literature, and art. But I do not find in his "Diary" any such passages as this, which Pepys writes on October 19, 1662 (Lord's day):

Put on my first new lace-band: and so neat it is, that I am resolved my great expense shall be lace-bands, and it will set off anything else the more. I am sorry to hear that the news of the selling of Dunkirk is taken so generally ill, as I find it is among the merchants; and other things, as removal of officers at Court, good for worse; and all things else made much worse in their report among people than they are. And this night, I know not upon what ground, the gates of the City ordered to be all shut, and double guards everywhere. Indeed I do find everybody's spirit very full of trouble: and the things of the Court and Council very ill taken; so as to be apt to appear in bad colours, if there should ever be a beginning of trouble, which God forbid!

Or,

29th (Lord's day).

This morning I put on my best black cloth suit, trimmed with scarlet ribbon, very neat, with my cloak lined with velvet, and a new beaver, which altogether is very noble, with my black silk knit canons I bought a month ago.

Evelyn never condescends to such weaknesses as we find in our beloved Pepys!

One wonders whether, if the noble Mr. Evelyn had been able to decipher some of the hidden things in Mr. Pepys's "Diary," he would have written this tribute, under the date of May 26, 1703:

This day died Mr. Sam Pepys, a very worthy, industrious and curious person.... He lived at Clapham with his partner, Mr. Hewer, formerly his clerk, in a very noble house and sweete place, where he enjoyed the fruite of his labours in greate prosperity. He was universally belov'd, hospitable, generous, learned in many things, skill'd in music, a very greate cherisher of learned men of whom he had the conversation. His library and collection of other curiosities were of the most considerable, the models of ships especially.... Mr. Pepys had been for neere 40 years so much my particular friend, that Mr. Jackson sent me compleat mourning, desiring me to be one to hold up the pall at his magnificent obsequies, but my indisposition hindered me from doing him this last office.

All the teachings of the histories of our student days force us to look on Charles II. as one of the weakest of English kings; but when we come to enjoy Pepys and to revere Evelyn, we begin to see that there is much to be said for him as a monarch, and that he did more for England under difficult circumstances than conventional history has given him credit for.

It took many years for me to find any diary or memoir that appealed to me as much as that of Pepys. His great charm is that he does for you what formal history never does; he takes you into the heart of his time, and introduces you into the centre of his mind and heart. In literature, in poetry and prose, the reader hopes that the roofs of houses or the tops of heads might be taken off, so that we could see with an understanding eye what goes on. The interest of the human race, though it may be disguised rhetorically, is the interest that everybody finds in gossip. Malicious gossip is one thing; but that gossip that makes us know our fellow men and women somewhat as we know ourselves—but perhaps more clearly—can never be rooted out of normal human nature.

I read and re-read favourite parts of Pepys's "Diary" many times, and I sat myself down in many cozy corners, on hills, on valleys, by land, and by sea, to dip into the "Memoirs of Saint-Simon"; and then there was always Madame de Sévigné. Much was hoped from the long-promised "Memoirs of Talleyrand." They came; they were disappointing.

Suddenly arrived a very complete and egoistical book that compares in a way with the perennial favourites of mine I have been writing about. And this is "The Education of Henry Adams," and almost contemporaneously the "Letters of William James." It is easy to understand the delight with which intelligent people welcomed "The Education of Henry Adams." Unconsciously to most of us, it showed elaborately what we talked about in our graduation essays and what we believed in a vague way—that education consists in putting value on the circumstances of life, and regarding each circumstance as a step either forward or backward in one's educational progress. This is the lesson which young Americans are taught by Harold Bell Wright and Gene Stratton-Porter; and which Samuel Smiles beat into the heads of the English. Henry Adams's lesson, however, is not taught in the same way at all. There is no preaching; it is a series of pictures, painted by a gentleman, with a sure hand, who looks on the phenomena of life as no other American has ever looked on them, or, at least, as no other American has ever expressed them. The judicious and the sensitive and the nicely discerning may shrink with horror from me when I say that I put at once "The Education of Henry Adams," for my delectation, beside the "Apologia pro Vita Sua" of Cardinal Newman!

There is the same delicate egoism in both; there is the same reasonable and well-bred reticence. There is one great difference, however; while Cardinal Newman ardently longs for truth and is determined to find it, Henry Adams seems not quite sure whether truth is worth searching for or not. And yet Henry Adams is more human, more interesting than Cardinal Newman, for, while Newman is almost purely intellectual and so much above the reach of most of us, Adams is merely intelligent—but intelligent enough to discern the richness of life, and mystical enough to long for a religious key to its meaning. Newman not only longs, but reasons and acts. It was not the definition of the unity of God that troubled Adams. It was the question of His personality. The existence of pain and wretchedness in the world was a bar to his understanding that a personal Christ should be equal in divinity with God, in fact, God Himself.

Newman, who was more spiritual, saw that pain was no barrier to faith in a personal God. I am speaking now only from my own point of view; others who like to read both Newman and Adams may look on this view as entirely negligible. What other American than Adams would have so loved without understanding the spirit of Saint Francis d'Assisi:

Vast swarms of Americans knew the Civil War only by school history, as they knew the story of Cromwell or Cicero, and were as familiar with political assassination as though they had lived under Nero. The climax of empire could be seen approaching, year after year, as though Sulla were a President or McKinley a Consul.

Nothing annoyed America more than to be told this simple and obvious— in no way unpleasant—truth; therefore one sat silent as ever on the Capitol; but, by way of completing the lesson, the Lodges added a pilgrimage to Assisi and an interview with St. Francis, whose solution of historical riddles seemed the most satisfactory—or sufficient—ever offered; worth fully forty years' more study, and better worth it than Gibbon himself, or even St. Augustine, St. Ambrose, or St. Jerome. The most bewildering effect of all these fresh crosslights on the old Assistant Professor of 1874 was due to the astonishing contrast between what he had taught them and what he found himself confusedly trying to learn five-and-twenty years afterwards—between the twelfth century of his thirtieth and that of his sixtieth years. At Harvard College, weary of spirit in the wastes of Anglo-Saxon law, he had occasionally given way to outbursts of derision at shedding his life-blood for the sublime truths of Sac and Soc:—

Hic Jacet
Homunculus Scriptor
Doctor Barbaricus
Henricus Adams
Adae Filius et Evae
Primo Explicuit
Socnam

The Latin was as twelfth century as the law, and he meant as satire the claim that he had been first to explain the legal meaning of Sac and Soc, although any German professor would have scorned it as a shameless and presumptuous bid for immortality; but the whole point of view had vanished in 1900. Not he, but Sir Henry Maine and Rudolph Sohm, were the parents or creators of Sac and Soc. Convinced that the clue of religion led to nothing, and that politics led to chaos, one had turned to the law, as one's scholars turned to the Law School, because one could see no other path to a profession.

The law had proved as futile as politics or religion, or any other single thread spun by the human spider; it offered no more continuity than architecture or coinage, and no more force of its own. St. Francis expressed supreme contempt for them all, and solved the whole problem by rejecting it altogether. Adams returned to Paris with a broken and contrite spirit, prepared to admit that his life had no meaning, and conscious that in any case it no longer mattered.

After all, the speculations of Henry Adams, his thrusts at philosophy, seem as futile as those of that very great American John Burroughs. It is the facts of life as seen through his personality, the changes in our political history as analyzed so skilfully by him after the manner of no other man that make his book supremely interesting.

The real man is not hidden in "The Education of Henry Adams." We can no longer talk of the degeneracy of American literary taste when we know that this very American, characteristic, and illuminating book was a "best seller" in our country for several months. Some who like to bewail the degeneracy of our art and literature and of our drama, declare that its popularity is simply due to a fashion. Biographies are the fashion, and therefore it is the transitory habit of the illiterate book buyer to purchase, if he does not read, biographies. This view may be dismissed with a scornful wave of the hand.

When I took up "The Education of Henry Adams," I was informed that it was "pathetic." Personally, it has never struck me that Henry Adams, as far as I know him, is at all pathetic. He did not assume an air of pathos when he read my review in *Scribner's Monthly*—before it became the *Century*—of the novel "Democracy." Mr. Richard Watson Gilder, the editor, was away at the time, and I recall his whimsical horror when on his return he read the things I had said about a novel, which I, in the heat of youth, held to be entirely un-American.

Mr. Henry Adams's book, in my opinion, has no element of pathos. Adams lived a rare and interesting life. He loved beauty, and was so prepared by tradition and education that he knew how to appreciate beauty wherever he found it, and to give reasons for its being beautiful. Against the rough material obstacles in life, which are supposed to be good for a man, but are not at all good, since they absorb a great deal of energy that is subtracted from his later life, he was not obliged to struggle. Like Theodore Roosevelt, the greatest of all modern Americans, who was a man of letters in love with life, Adams was not compelled to look up to social strata above him, and, whatever the enraged democrats may say, this in itself is a great advantage. One can see from his "Education" that his material difficulties were so slight that he could take them cheerfully, even in our world where poverty is both a blunder and a crime. This in itself tends toward happiness. Henry Adams, it is true, suffered terribly in his heart. His description of the death of his sister is heart-rending; he does not dwell on the worst of his griefs. No man had a more agreeable circle of friends, no man more pleasant surrounding. He was free in a way that few other men are free, and to my mind it is this sense of freedom, of which he does not always take advantage, that is one of the most appealing qualities of his book. It is a great relief to meet a man and to be intimate with him, as we are with Henry Adams, who has the power of using wings, whether he uses them or not.

There are many reasons for the success of his book. The chapters on "Diplomacy," on "Friends and Foes," on "Political Morality," and on "The Battle of the Rams" are new contributions to our history. More than that, they elucidate conditions of mind which are generally wrapped up, for motives of policy, in misty and often hypocritical verbiage.

Some of the reviewers found "The Education" egotistical. This is too strong a term. These memoirs would have no value if they were not egotistical; and if the term "egotistical" implies conceit or self-complacency or the desire to show one's better side to the public, "The Education" does not deserve it. A man cannot write about himself without writing about himself. This seems very much like a platitude. And Henry Adams writes about himself with no affectation of modesty. If anything, he underrates himself, as in conversation he sometimes took a tone which made him appear to those who knew him slightly as below the average of the real Henry Adams.

Here, for instance, is a good passage:

Swinburne tested him [Henry Adams] then and there by one of his favourite tests—Victor Hugo; for to him the test of Victor Hugo was the surest and quickest of standards. French poetry is at best a severe exercise for foreigners; it requires extraordinary knowledge of the language and rare refinement of ear to appreciate even the recitation of French verse; but unless a poet has both, he lacks something of poetry. Adams had neither. To the end of his life he never listened to a French recitation with pleasure, or felt a sense of majesty in French verse; but he did not care to proclaim his weakness, and he tried to evade Swinburne's vehement insistence by parading an affection for Alfred de Musset. Swinburne would have none of it; De Musset was unequal; he did not sustain himself on the wing.

Adams would have given a world or two, if he owned one, to sustain himself on the wing like De Musset, or even like Hugo; but his education as well as his ear was at fault, and he succumbed. Swinburne tried him again on Walter Savage Landor. In truth the test was the same, for Swinburne admired in Landor's English the qualities that he felt in Hugo's French; and Adams's failure was equally gross, for, when forced to despair, he had to admit that both Hugo and Landor bored him. Nothing more was needed. One who could feel neither Hugo nor Landor was lost.

The sentence was just and Adams never appealed from it. He knew his inferiority in taste as he might know it in smell. Keenly mortified by the dullness of his senses and instincts, he knew he was no companion for Swinburne; probably he could be only an annoyance; no number of centuries could ever educate him to Swinburne's level, even in technical appreciation; yet he often wondered whether there was nothing he had to offer that was worth the poet's acceptance. Certainly such mild homage as the American insect would have been only too happy to bring, had he known how, was hardly worth the acceptance of any one. Only in France is the attitude of prayer possible; in England it became absurd. Even Monckton Milnes, who felt the splendours of Hugo and Landor, was almost as helpless as an American private secretary in personal contact with them. Ten years afterwards Adams met him at the Geneva Conference, fresh from Paris, bubbling with delight at a call he had made on Hugo; "I was shown into a large room," he said, "with women and men seated in chairs against the walls, and Hugo at one end throned. No one spoke. At last Hugo raised his voice solemnly, and uttered the words: "Quant a moi, je crois en Dieu!" Silence followed. Then a woman responded as if in deep meditation: "Chose sublime! un Dieu qui croit en Dieu!"

The *Chose sublime* is an Adamesque touch! It gives the last delicate tint to the impression. Page after page gleams with such impressions and such touches. He looks deep, and he sees clearly. But he lacks faith! He is the discoverer of the twelfth century; and, in a lesser sense, the discoverer of the real meaning of the nineteenth. He perceived the real architecture of both the Cathedral of Chartres and of "The Song of Roland." How useless all the tomes of the learned Teutons seem in comparison with his volume on Chartres, and their conclusions are so laboured and ineffective in comparison with the lightning-like glance with which he pierces the real meaning of the twelfth century. He has his limitations, and he is not unaware of them. But when one reflects on the hideous self-complacency, the eighteenth-century ignorance, the half-educated vulgarity of most of the writers in German and English who pretend to interpret the Middle Ages, one cannot help giving grateful thanks for having found Henry Adams.

To be sure, he does not respect Harvard, and one of his reasons seems to be that the Harvard man, though capable of valuing the military architecture of the walls of Constantinople, cannot sympathize with the beauties of Chartres or Sancta Sophia. Yale, he assumes, is more receptive. However, Henry Adams, if he were alive to-day, would have discovered that both Yale and Harvard, both seekers after culture and the cultivated, the hitherto prejudiced and self-opinionated, have profited greatly by the education he has given them. It seems that Henry Adams fancied that he had failed as an educator. He did not realize that he would give his countrymen an education which they greatly lacked, and which many of them are sincerely grateful for.

The man that cannot read his chapter on "Eccentricity" over and over again is incapable of appreciating some of Pepys's best passages! Books to be read and re-read ought to occupy only a small space on any shelf, and not many of them, in my opinion, are among the One Hundred Best Books listed by the late Sir John Lubbock. Each of us will make his own shelf of books. The book for me is the book that delights, attracts, soothes, or uplifts me. Let those critics go hang whose criticisms are not literature! Sainte-Beuve makes literature when he exercises his critical vocation; Brunetière has too heavy a hand; Francisque Sarcey has some touches of inspiration that give delight. There are no really good French critics to-day, probably because they have so little material to work on. Our own Mencken, with all his vagaries, is worth while, and Brander Matthews knows his line and the value of background and perspective; William Lyon Phelps has a light hand; but there are many leaves in our forests of critical writing and not much wood. Literary criticism is becoming a lost art with our English brethren, who once claimed Saintsbury and George Lewes. The admitted existence of cliques and claques in London makes us distrustful. You were worked into great enthusiasm for Stephen Phillips's "Herod" until you found that half a score of notices of this tragedy were written by the same hand!

It seems almost impossible that "The Letters of William James" should appear shortly after "The Education of Henry Adams," and, though the Jameses were New Yorkers, they are certainly redolent of New England. We had begun to forget our debt to the writers of New England. Mrs. Freeman and Mr. Lincoln hold up their heads as writers of modern folk stories; but the *Atlantic Monthly* has become eclectic. It has lost the flavour of New England. That Boston which in the *Atlantic* had always been a state of mind has become different from the real old Boston.

In truth, Indiana had begun to blot out the whole of New England, and Miss Agnes Repplier had begun to stain our map of culture with the modulated tints of Philadelphia. For myself, I had returned to the novels of Harriet Beecher Stowe—leaving out "Uncle Tom's Cabin," which I always found detestable—to "Elsie Venner" and to "The Autocrat of the Breakfast Table," in the hope that the flavour of New England, which I found to my horror was growing faint in me, might be retained. There is always "The House of the Seven Gables!"

But, while I was lingering over some almost forgotten pages of Mrs. Stowe with great pleasure, something she said reminded me of Walter Savage

Landor, and I turned to the only work of Landor which had ever attracted me, "The Imaginary Conversations." There was an interlude of enjoyment and exasperation. He shows himself so malicious, so bigoted, so narrow, and so incapable of comprehending some of the historical persons he presents to us. But there are compensations, all the same. Whatever one may think of the animus of Landor, one cannot get on without an occasional dip into "The Imaginary Conversations." Suddenly Landor reminded me of Marion Crawford's "With the Immortals," and I rediscovered Marion Crawford's Heinrich Heine! To have discovered Heine in Zangwill's "In a Mattress Grave" was worth a long search through many magazines. Like Stevenson's "Lodging for the Night," Zangwill's few pages can never be obliterated from the heart of a loving reader—by a loving reader I mean a reader who loves men a little more than books.

You will remember that Crawford's Immortals appear at Sorrento where Lady Brenda and Augustus and Gwendolyn Chard are enjoying the fine flower of life. If Sir Conan Doyle and Sir Oliver Lodge could only bring back to life, or induce to come back to life, King Francis I. and Julius Cæsar and Heinrich Heine and Doctor Johnson,[1] together with that group of semi-happy souls who live on the "enamelled green" of Dante, spiritism might have more to say for itself!

"'I call a cat a cat,' as Boileau put it," remarked Heine. "I would like to know how many men in a hundred are disappointed in the women they marry."

"Just as many as have too much imagination," said Augustus.

"No," said Johnson, shaking his head violently and speaking suddenly in an excited tone. "No. Those who are disappointed are such as are possessed of imagination without judgment; but a man whose imagination does not outrun his judgment is seldom deceived in the realisation of his hopes. I suspect that the same thing is true in the art of poetry, of which Herr Heine is at once a master and a judge. For the qualities that constitute genius are invention, imagination and judgment; invention, by which new trains of events are formed, and new scenes of imagery displayed; imagination, which strongly impresses on the writer's mind, and enables him to convey to the reader the various form of nature, incidents of life and energies of passion; and judgment, which selects from life or nature what the present purpose requires, and by separating the essence of things from its concomitants, often makes the representation more powerful than the reality. A man who possesses invention and imagination can invent and imagine a thousand beauties, gifts of mind and virtues of character; but unless he have judgment which enables him to discern the bounds of possibility and to detect the real nature of the woman he has chosen as the representative of his self-formed ideal, he runs great risk of being deceived. As a general rule, however, it has pleased Providence to endow man with much more judgment than imagination; and to this cause we may attribute the small number of poets who have flourished in the world, and the great number of happy marriages among civilised mankind."

"It appears that I must have possessed imagination after all," said Francis.

"If you will allow me to say it," said Cæsar in his most suave tones, and turning his heavy black eyes upon the king's face, "you had too much. Had you possessed less imagination and more judgment, you might many times have destroyed the Emperor Charles. To challenge him to fight a duel was a gratuitous and very imaginative piece of civility; to let him escape as you did more than once when you could easily have forced an engagement on terms advantageous to yourself, was unpardonable."

"I know it," said Francis, bitterly. "I was not Cæsar."

"No, sir," said Johnson in loud, harsh tones, "nor were you happy in your marriages—"

"I adore learned men," whispered Francis to Lady Brenda. He had at once recovered his good humour.

"A fact that proves what I was saying, that the element of judgment is necessary in the selection of a wife," continued the doctor.

"I think it is intuition which makes the right people fall in love with each other," said Lady Brenda.

"Intuition, madam," replied Johnson, "means the mental view; as you use it you mean a very quick and accurate mental view, followed immediately by an unconscious but correct process of deduction. The combination of the two, when they are nicely adjusted, constitutes a kind of judgment which, though it be not always so correct in its conclusions, as that exercised by ordinary logic, has nevertheless the advantage of quickness combined with tolerable precision. For, in matters of love, it is necessary to be quick."

"Who sups with the devil must have a long spoon," said Francis, laughing.

"And he who hopes to entertain an angel must keep his house clean," returned the doctor.

"Do you believe that people always fall in love very quickly?" asked Lady Brenda.

"Frequently, though not always. Love dominates quite as much because its attacks are sudden and unexpected, as because most persons believe that to be in love is a desirable state."

"Love," said Cæsar, "is a great general and a great strategist, for he rarely fails to surprise the enemy if he can, but he never refuses an open engagement when necessary."

Strange as it may appear, it does not seem to be so much of a descent, or of a break in the chain of continuity, to turn to hear William James speak in letters, which have the effect of conversation. From the very beginning of his precious book I somehow feel that I am part of the little circle about him. The conversation goes on—Mr. James never loses sight of the point of view and sympathies of the party of the second part—and you are not made to feel as an eavesdropper.

Standing on the ladder, unhappily a rather shaky ladder, to put back "With the Immortals" on the shelf, I pass Wells's great novel of "Marriage," which I would clutch to read again, if I had not already begun this Letter of James— written to his wife:

I have often thought that the best way to define a man's character would be to seek out the particular mental or moral attitude in which, when it came upon him, he felt himself most deeply and intensely active and alive. At such moments there is a voice inside which speaks and says: "This is the real me!" And afterwards, considering the circumstances in which the man is placed, and noting how some of them are fitted to evoke this attitude, whilst others do not call for it, an outside observer may be able to prophesy where the man may fail, where succeed, where be happy and where miserable. Now as well as I can describe it, this characteristic attitude in me always involves an element of active tension, of holding my own, as it were, and trusting outward things to perform their part so as to make it a full harmony, but without any *guaranty* that they will. Make it a guaranty—and the attitude immediately becomes to my consciousness stagnant and stingless. Take away the guaranty, and I feel (provided I am *überhaupt* in vigorous condition) a sort of deep enthusiastic bliss, of bitter willingness to do and suffer anything, which translates itself physically by a kind of stinging pain inside my breastbone (don't smile at this—it is to me an essential element of the whole thing!), and which, although it is a mere mood or emotion to which I can give no form in words, authenticates itself to me as the deepest principle of all active and theoretic determination which I possess....

Personal expression is, after all, what we long for in literature. Cardinal Newman tells us, I think, in his "Idea of a University," that it *is* the very essence of literature. *Scientia* is truth, or conclusions stated as truths which stand irrespective of the personality of the speaker or writer. But literature, to be literature, must be personal. It is good literature when it is expressed plastically, and in accordance with a good usage of its time. A reader like myself does not, perhaps, trouble himself sufficiently with the philosophy of

William James as represented in these "Letters." One has a languid interest in knowing what he thought of Bergson and Nietzsche or even of Hegel; but for the constant reader his detachment or attachment to Aristotle and St. Thomas Aquinas is not nearly so important as his personal impressions of both the little things and the big things of our contemporary life. Whether you are pragmatic or not, you must, if you are at all in love with life, become a Jamesonian after you have read the "Letters"! And his son, Mr. Henry James, who, we may hope, may resemble his father in time, has arranged them so well, and kept himself so tactfully in the background, that you feel, too, that whether young Henry is a pragmatist or not, he is a most understanding human being. The only way to read these "Letters" is to dip into them here and there, as the only way to make a good salad is to pour the vinegar on drop by drop. To use an oriental metaphor, the oil of appreciation is stimulated by the acid of wit, the salt of wisdom, and the pepper of humour. Frankly, since I discovered William James as a human being I have begun to read him for the same reason that I read Pepys—for pure enjoyment!

A friend of mine, feeling that I had taken the "Letters of William James" too frivolously, told me that I ought to go to Mr. Wells to counteract my mediæval philosophy and too cheerful view of life. Just as if I had not struggled with Mr. Wells, and irritated myself into a temperature in trying to get through his latest preachments! I am not quite sure what I said of Mr. Wells, but I find, in an article by Mr. Desmond MacCarthy in the "New Statesman," just what I ought to have said.

This doctrine of the inspired priesthood of authors is exaggerated and dangerous. Neither has it, you see, prevented him from writing "The Wonderful Visit." Artists should feel, and if necessary be told, that they are on their honour to do their best. That will do. If they flatter themselves that they are messengers from the Father of Light whenever they put pen to paper, they are apt to take any emotional hubble-bubble in themselves as a sign that the Spirit has been brooding upon the waters, and pour out; though a short time afterwards they may let loose a spate flowing in a quite different direction. Sincerity of the moment is not sincerity; those who have watched England's prime minister know that.

William James helped me to wash the bad taste of Mr. Wells's god out of my mouth. It seems remarkable that such a distinguished man of talent—if he were dead, one would be justified in saying a man of genius—should not have been able to invent a more attractive and potent Deity. Voltaire, while making no definition, did better than that; but Voltaire was a much cleverer man than Wells, and he had an education such as no modern writer has. When Mr. Wells preaches, he becomes a bore. Who, except the empty-minded, or those who, like the Athenians, are always seeking new things, can take Mr. Wells's dogmatisms seriously? Is it not in one of his "Sermones" that Horace tells us that the merchant wants to be a sailor and the sailor a merchant? Does he not begin with—*Qui fit, Mæcenas?* But Horace says nothing of the authors of fiction—Stevenson calls them very lightly "*filles de joie*,"—who insist on being boldly and brutally theologians and philosophers. Horace might have invented a better god than Wells; but he had too much good taste and too much knowledge of man in the world to attempt it.

The more one reads of the very moderns, the more one falls in love with the ancients. Take the peerless Horatius Flaccus, for instance. Do you think anybody would read his Odes and Epodes and love him as we do if he insisted that we should "sit under him" and assumed a pulpit manner? This is as near as he ever comes to teaching us anything:

Lenit albescens animos capillus
Litium et rixae cupidos protervae
;Non ego hoc ferrem calidus juventa,
Consule Planco.

Even Sir Edward Bulwer-Lytton, who loved himself very much, showed in his translations of "The Odes and Epodes" that he could almost love something as well as himself. It does not become me to recommend books—everybody to his own taste!—but I should like to say that for those whose Latin has become only a faint perfume of attar of roses, like that which is said to cling faintly to one of the desks of Marie Antoinette at Versailles, the translations of our dear Horatius by Lord Lytton is a very precious aid to a knowledge of one of the most charming and most wise of pagan poets.

Horace says:

Postumus, Postumus, the years glide by us,
Alas! no piety delays the wrinkles,
Nor old age imminent,
Nor the indomitable hand of Death.

We might have, in spite of the awful examples of Mr. Wells and the other preachers, who ought to confine themselves to finer things, desired that Horace should have gone further and told us what kind of books we ought to read in our old age. His choice was naturally limited; it was impossible for him to buy a book every week, or every month. The publishers were not so active in those days. But he might have indicated the kind of book that old age might read, in order to renew its youth. I have tried "Robinson Crusoe,"—the unequalled—and "Swiss Family Robinson"; but they seem too grown up for me now. I have taken to "King Solomon's Mines" and

"Treasure Island" and that perfect gem of excitement and illusion, "The Mutineers," by Charles Boardman Hawes. I read it, and I'm young again. I trust that some enterprising bookseller will unblushingly compile a library for the old, and begin it with "The Mutineers!" The main difficulty with the Old or the Near Old is that the fear of shocking the Young makes them such hypocrites. They pretend that they like Mr. Wells and the other preachers; they express intense interest in new and ponderous books, in the presence of Youth—when they ought to yawn frankly and bury themselves in romances. But if the Old really want to save their faces, and at the same time enjoy glimpses of that fountain of youth which we long for at every age, let them acquire two books—Clifford Smyth's "The Gilded Man" and "The Quest of El Dorado," by Dr. J. A. Zahm, whose *nom de plume* was H. J. Mozans. There you have the real stuff. Together, these two books are a combination of just what the Old need to found dreams on. If a man does not smoke he cannot dream with any facility when he grows old; and if he has not possessed himself of these two volumes, he cannot have acquired that basis for dreams which the energetic Aged greatly need. "The Gilded Man" is frankly a romance, and yet, strangely enough, a romance of facts, and "The Quest of El Dorado" is the only volume in the English language when it deals with the El Dorado; it has all the most attractive qualities of a romance.

But they are not enough. To them I add, "Bob, Son of Battle," which the author of "Alice For Short," discovered late in life. It is the greatest animal-human story ever written, for Owd Bob is nobly human, and the Black Killer devilishly human, and yet they are dogs; not fabulous dogs, invented by clever writers. A great book! It is too thrilling; it reminds of "Wuthering Heights"; I shall, therefore, read this evening some of Henry Van Dyke's Canadian stories, and end the day with "Pride and Prejudice."

[1]

"*Cola diritto, sopra il verde smalto
mi fur moetrati gli spiriti magni
che del verderli in me stesso 'n esalto*"

—INFERNO.

CHAPTER V

BOOKS AT RANDOM

Among nature books that gave me many happy hours on the banks of the Delaware—imperial river!—is Charles C. Abbott's "Upland and Meadow." "Better," Mr. Abbott says, "repeat the twelve labours of Hercules than attempt to catalogue the varied forms of life found in the area of an average ramble!" *Soit!* And better than that, "to feel that whatever creature we may meet will prove companionable—that is, no stranger, but rather an amusing and companionable friend—assures both pleasure and profit whenever we chance abroad."

Who that has made "Upland and Meadow" his companion can forget the extracts from the diary of the Ancient Man, dated Ninth Month, 1734, in the Delaware Valley? Noisy guns had reduced the number of wild ducks and geese, he says, even then. But, nevertheless, Watson's Creek was often black with the smaller fowl.

I do seldom see the great swans, but father says that they are not unusual in the wide stretches of the Delaware.

Happy day! when the wedge-shaped battalions of wild geese were almost as frequently seen as the spattering sparrows now!

Father allowed me [writes the good Quaker boy, in 1734] to accompany my Indian friend, Oconio, to Watson's creek, that we may gather wild fowl after the Indian manner. With great eagerness, I accompanied Oconio, and thus happened it. We did reach the widest part of that creek early in the morning, I think the sun was scarcely an half-hour high. Oconio straightway hid himself in the tall grass by the water, while I was bidden to lie in the tall grass at a little distance. With his bow and arrows, Oconio quickly shot a duck that came near, by swimming within a short distance of him. I marvelled much with what skill he shot, for his arrow pierced the head of the duck which gave no alarming cry.... Oconio now did fashion a circlet of green boughs, and so placed them about his head and shoulders that I saw not his face; he otherwise disrobed and walked into the stream. He held in one hand a shotten duck, so that it swam lustily, and, so equipped, was in the midst of a cluster of fowl, of which he deftly seized several so quickly that their fellows took no alarm. These he strangled beneath the water, and, when he had three of them, came back with caution to where the thick bushes concealed him. He desired that I should do the same, and with much hesitation I disrobed and assumed the disguise Oconio had fashioned; then I put forth boldly towards the gathered fowl, at which they did arise with a great clamour, and were gone. I marvel much why this should have been, but Oconio did not make it clear, and I forbore, through foolish pride, to ask him. And let it not be borne in mind against me [pleads the good Quaker boy] that, when I reached my home, I wandered to the barn, and writing an ugly word upon the door, sat long and gazed at it. Chagrin doth make me feel very meek, I find, but I set no one an example by speech or act, in thus soothing my feelings in so worldly a manner.

This example may be commended to players of golf, who are inclined to be "worldly." The episode of Oconio at the best is too long to quote; it, too, has its lesson! One reads Mr. Abbott's defence of the skunk cabbage, for it harbours at its root

the earliest salamanders, the pretty Maryland yellow throat nests in the hollows of its broad leaves, and rare beetles find a congenial home in the shelter it affords.

"Upland and Meadow" gives one occasion for thought on the subject of raccoons. "Foolish creatures, like opossums, thrive while cunning coons are forced to quest or die."

For a stroll by the Thames—I mean the New England Thames—there is no book like Ik Marvel's "Dream Life," but for a day near the Delaware—imperial river!—give me "Upland and Meadow."

And then with what assurance of satisfaction may one turn for refreshment to the continual charm of John Burroughs's books, "Riverby" and "Pepacton." Burroughs's opinions upon the problems of humanity are more tiresome than John Bunyan's opinions on theology; but to go with him among the birds and the plants, to hope with him that the soaring lark of England may find its way down through Canada to our hedges, to look with him into the nests in the shrubs that border our roads is to begin to feel that joy in being an American of the soil that no other author gives. He cured the young New England poets and the singers of the Berkshire Hills and of the Catskills of celebrating the English thrush and the nightingale, as if those birds sang on the Palisades.

There is an epithet I should like to apply to John Burroughs, but he might not like it if he were alive. I recall the case of a pleasant Englishman who admired two American girls very much, because, as he said, they were "so homely." In fact, they were rather pretty girls, and he had not used the term in reference to their looks. It is the word with which I like to describe John Burroughs. Forty years ago, I met him at Richard Watson Gilder's. He was young then, and delightfully "homely" in the sense in which the Englishman used the word. Some of the refined ladies at Mrs. Gilder's objected to his "crude speech," for even in the eighties there were still *précieuses*. The truth is that his rural use of the vernacular was part of the charm. It never spoiled his style; but it gave that touch of homeliness to it which smelt of the good soil of the country.

Thoreau's "Walden" always reminds me—a far-fetched comparison but I will not apologize for it—of "As You Like It" played in one way by Dybwad, the Norwegian actress, and by Julia Marlowe in another. Madame Dybwad, being nearer to the Elizabethan time in her daily life, gives us an Elizabethan maiden with a touch of "homeliness"; but Julia Marlowe's, like Ada Rehan's "Rosalind," has something of the artificial character of Watteau. "Walden," then, is somewhat too varnished; but "Riverby" and "Pepacton" are "homely" and "homey."

To return to memoirs for a moment, that most delightful of all mental dissipations for a leisurely man. In looking for the second volume of "Walden"—for fear that I should have done Thoreau an injustice—I find the "Memoirs of the Comtesse de Boigne." One cannot imagine anything more unlike Madame de Boigne than Thoreau and John Burroughs! Why is Madame de Boigne on the same shelf with these two lovers of nature? Madame de Boigne was never a lover of nature. She loved the world and the manifestations of the world, and—not to be ungallant—she is more like an irritated mosquito than like the elegant *camellia japonica* to which she would prefer to be compared.

There is a great deal of solid comfort in the revelations of Madame de Boigne; she is at times so very untruthful that her malice does no real harm; she is so very clever; and she paints interiors so well; and gives the atmosphere of French Society before and during the Revolution in a most fascinating way. She always thinks the worst, of course; but a writer of memoirs who always thought the best would be as painfully uninteresting as Froude is when he describes the character of Henry VIII. But this is a digression.

Mr. John Addington Symonds speaks of the style of Sir Thomas Browne as displaying a "rich maturity and heavy-scented blossom." Mr. Mencken cannot accuse any modern Englishman or American of imitating, in his desire to be academic, Browne's hyperlatinism or his use of Latin words, like "corpage," "confinium," "angustias," or "Vivacious abominations" and "congaevous generations."

Mr. Symonds says:

He professes a mixture of the boldest scepticism and the most puerile credulity. But his scepticism is the prelude to confessions of impassioned faith, and his credulity is the result of tortuous reflections on the enigmas of life and revelation. Perhaps the following paragraph enables us to understand the permanent temper of his mind most truly:

"As for those wingy mysteries in divinity, and airy subtleties in religion, which have unhinged the brains of better heads, they never stretched the pia mater of mine. Methinks there be not impossibilities enough in religion for an active faith: the deepest mysteries ours contains have not only been illustrated but maintained by syllogism and the rule of reason. I love to lose myself in a mystery; to pursue my reason to an O altitudo! 'Tis my solitary recreation to pose my apprehension with those involved enigmas and riddles of the Trinity, Incarnation, and Resurrection. I can answer all the objections of Satan and my rebellious reason with that odd resolution I learned of Tertullian, *Certum est quia impossible est*. I desire to exercise my faith in the difficultest point, for to credit ordinary and visible objects, is not faith, but persuasion."

Leaving all question of theology, or criticism of theology, aside, Sir Thomas lends himself to those moments when a man wants to dip a little into the interior life. It is a strange thing that nearly all the modern novelists who describe men seem to think that their interior life is purely emotional. Even Mr. Hugh Walpole,[2] my favourite among the writers in the spring of middle age, is inclined to make his heroes, or his semi-heroes (there are no good real honest villains in fiction now) lead lives that are not at all interior. And yet every man either leads an interior life, or longs to lead an interior life, of which he seldom talks. He wants inarticulately to know something of the art of meditation; his dissatisfaction with life, even when he is successful, is largely due to the fact that he has never been taught how to cultivate the spiritual sense. This is an art. In it St. Francis de Sales was very proficient. It gave George Herbert and a group of his imitators great contentment in the state to which they were called. As a book of secular meditation the "Religio Medici" is full of good points. For instance, Sir Thomas starts one on the road to meditation on the difference between democracy and freedom, humanity and nationalism in this way:

Let us speak like politicians; there is a nobility without heraldry, a natural dignity, whereby one man is ranked with another filed before him, according to the quality of his desert and pre-eminence of his good parts. Though the corruption of these times and the bias of present practice wheel another way, thus it was in the first and primitive commonwealths, and is yet in the integrity and cradle of well-ordered politics: till corruption getteth ground;— ruder desires labouring after that which wiser considerations contemn;— every one having a liberty to amass and heap up riches, and they a license or faculty to do or purchase anything.

There are singular beings who have tried to read "Religio Medici" continuously. Was it Shakespeare, whose works were presented to one of this class? "How do you like Shakespeare?" the amiable donor asked. "I can't say yet; I have not finished him!" It seems almost miraculous that human beings should exist who take this attitude toward Sir Thomas Browne, his "Urn Burial" or his "Christian Morals." It seems almost more miraculous that this attitude should be taken toward Montaigne, and that some folk should prefer the "Essays of Montaigne" in the pleasant, curtailed edition of John Florio's translation, edited by Justin Huntly McCarthy! These small books are convenient, no doubt. If you cannot have the original French, or the leisure to browse over the big volume of Florio's old book as it was written, Mr. McCarthy's edition is an agreeable but not satisfactory substitute. It somehow or other reminds one of that appalling series of cutdown "Classics," so largely recommended to a public that is seduced to run and read. A condensed edition of Froissart may do very well for boys; but who can visualize the kind of mind content with a reduced version of "Vanity Fair"?

Montaigne is a city of refuge from the whirling words of the uplifters. At times I have been compelled from a sense of duty, a mistaken one, to read whole pages of Mr. Wells, whose "Marriage" and "The New Machiavelli" and "Tono-Bungay," will be remembered when "Mr. Britling"—by the way, what did Mr. Britling see through?—shall be forgotten. As an antidote, I invariably turn to Montaigne. It amazed me to hear Montaigne called a skeptic. He is even more reverent toward the eternal verities than Sir Thomas Browne, and he has fewer superstitions. It was his humanity and his love for religion that turned him from Aristotle to Plato, and yet he is no fanatic for Plato. He is a real amateur of good books. Listen to this:

As for Cicero, I am of the common judgment, that besides learning there was an exquisite eloquence in him: He was a good citizen, of an honest, gentle nature, as are commonly fat and burly men: for so was he. But to speak truly of him, full of ambitious vanity and remisse niceness. And I know not well how to excuse him, in that he deemed his Poesie worthy to be published. It is no great imperfection to make bad verses, but it is an imperfection in him that he never perceived how unworthy they were of the glorie of his name. Concerning his eloquence it is beyond all comparison, and I verily believe that none shall ever equal it.

Montaigne sorrowed it a thousand times that ever the book written by Brutus on Virtue was lost. He consoles himself, however, by remembering that Brutus is so well represented in Plutarch. He would rather know what talk Brutus had with some of his familiar friends in his tent on the night before going to battle than the speech he made to his army. He had no sympathy with eloquent prefaces, or with circumlocutions that keep the reader back from the real matter of books. He does not want to hear heralds or criers. How he would have hated the flare of trumpets that precedes the entrance of the best sellers! And the blazing "jackets," the lowest form of modern art, would have made him rip out the favourite oaths of his province with violence.

"The Romans in their religion," he says, "were wont to say 'Hoc age'; which in ours we say, 'Sursum corda.'"

He goes to a book as he goes to a good dinner; he does not care for the *hors d'œuvres*. Note how he rushes with rather rough weapons to the translation, by his dying father's command, of *Theologia naturalis sive liber creaturarum magistri Raimondi de Sebonde*. He thinks that it is a good antidote for the "new fangles" of Luther, who is leading the vulgar to think for themselves and to reject authority. His analysis of himself in the essay "Of Cruelty" is the message of a sane man to sane men; and he does not hesitate to point out the fact that no hatred is so absolute as that which Christians can cover with the cloak of Christianity. The discord between zeal for religion and the fury of nationality concerns him greatly, and he does not hesitate to read a well-deserved lesson to his contemporaries on the subject.

In Montaigne's time the theories which Machiavelli had gathered together in "The Prince," governed Europe. One can see that they do not satisfy Montaigne. To him they are nefarious.

"'The Prince,'" declares Villari, "had a more direct action on real life than any other book in the world, and a larger share in emancipating Europe from the Middle Ages."

It is a shocking confession to make, and yet the "Essays" of Michel de Montaigne give me as much pleasure, but not so much edification, as the precious sentences of Thomas à Kempis. They are foils; at first sight there seems to be no relationship between them; and yet at heart Michel de Montaigne, who was really not a skeptic, has much in common with Thomas à Kempis. If there were no persons in the world capable of being Montaignes, Thomas à Kempis would have written for God alone. He would have resembled an altar railing which I once heard Father Faber had erected. On the side toward the altar it was foliated and exquisitely carved in a manner that pleased Ruskin. On the outer side, the side toward the people and not the side toward the Presence of God, it was entirely plain and unornamented!

The friendship of Thomas à Kempis I owe to George Eliot. Emerson might easily perish; Plato might go, and even Horace be drowned in his last supply of Falernian; Marcus Aurelius and even Rudyard Kipling might exist only in tradition; but the loss of all their works would be as nothing compared to the loss of that little volume which is a marvellous guide to life. The translations of Thomas à Kempis into English vary in value. Certain dissenters have cut out the very soul of À Kempis in deleting the passages on the Holy Eucharist. Think of Bowdlerizing Thomas à Kempis! He was, above all, a mystic, and all the philosophy of his love of Christ limps when the mystical centre of it, the Eucharist, is cut out. If that meeting in the upper room had not taken place during the paschal season, if Christ had not offered His body and blood, soul and divinity to his amazed, yet reverent, disciples, Thomas à Kempis would never have written "The Following of Christ." The Bible, even the New Testament, is full of sayings which, as St. James says of St. Paul's Epistles, are not easy sayings, but what better interpretation of the doctrines of Christ as applied to everyday life can there be found than in this precious little book?

You may talk of Marcus Aurelius and gather what comfort you can from the philosophy of Thoreau's "Walden"—which might, after all, be more comfortable if it were more pagan. The Pan of Thoreau was a respectable Pan, because he was a Unitarian; you may find some comfort in Keble's "Christian Year" if you can; but À Kempis overtops all! It is strange, too, what an appeal this great mystic has to the unbelievers in Christianity. It is a contradiction we meet with every day. And George Eliot was a remarkable example of this, for, in spite of her habitual reverence, she cannot be said to have accepted orthodox dogmas. Another paradox seems to be in the fact that Thomas à Kempis appeals so directly and consciously to the confirmed mystic and to those who have secluded themselves from the world. At first, I must confess that I found this a great obstacle to my joy in having found him.

If Montaigne frequently drove me to À Kempis, À Kempis almost as frequently in the beginning drove me back to Montaigne. It was not until I had become more familiar with the New Testament that I began to see that À Kempis spoke as one soul to another. In this world for him there were only three Facts—God, his own soul, and the soul to whom he spoke.

It was a puzzle to me to observe that so many of my friends who looked on the Last Supper as a mere symbol of love and hospitality, should cling to "The Following of Christ" with such devotion. Even the example of an intellectual friend of mine, a Bostonian who had lived much in Italy, could not make it clear. He often asserted that he did not believe in God; and yet he was desolate if on a certain day in the year he did not pay some kind of tribute at the shrine of St. Antony of Padua!

I have known him to break up a party in the Adirondacks in order to reach the nearest church where it was possible for him to burn a candle in honour of his favourite saint on this mysterious anniversary! As long as he exists, as long as he continues to burn candles—*les chandelles d'un athée*—I shall accept without understanding the enthusiasm of so many lovers of À Kempis, who cut out the mystical longings for the reception of that divine food which Christ gave out in the upper room. À Kempis says:

My soul longs to be nourished with Thy body; my heart desires to be united with Thee.

Give Thyself to me and it is enough; for without Thee no comfort is available.

Without Thee I cannot subsist; and without Thy visitation I cannot live.

And, therefore, I must come often to Thee, and receive Thee for the remedy, and for the health and strength of my soul; lest perhaps I faint in the way, if I be deprived of this heavenly food.

For so, O most merciful Jesus, Thou wast pleased once to say, when Thou hadst been preaching to the people, and curing sundry diseases: "I will not send them away fasting, lest they faint in the way."

Deal now in like manner with me, who has left Thyself in the sacrament for the comfort of Thy faithful.

For Thou art the most sweet reflection of the soul; and he that shall eat Thee worthily shall be partaker and heir of everlasting glory.

To every soul, oppressed and humble, À Kempis speaks more poignantly than even David, in that great cry of the heart and soul, the De Profundis:

Behold, then, O Lord, my abjection and frailty [Ps. xxiv. 18], every way known to Thee.

Have pity on me and draw me out of the mire [Ps. lxviii. 15], that I stick not fast therein, that I may not be utterly cast down forever.

This it is which often drives me back and confounds me in Thy sight, to find that I am so subject to fall and have so little strength to resist my passions.

And although I do not altogether consent, yet their assaults are troublesome and grievous to me, and it is exceedingly irksome to live thus always in a conflict.

Hence my infirmity is made known to me, because wicked thoughts do always much more easily rush in upon me than they can be cast out again.

Oh, that Thou, the most mighty God of Israel, the zealous lover of faithful souls, wouldst behold the labour and sorrow of Thy servant, and stand by me in all my undertakings.

Strengthen me with heavenly fortitude, lest the old man, the miserable flesh, not fully subject to the spirit, prevail and get the upper hand, against which we must fight as long as we breathe in this most wretched life.

Alas! what kind of life is this, where afflictions and miseries are never wanting; where all things are full of snares and enemies.

There is no pessimism here, for Thomas à Kempis gives the remedies, the only remedies offered to the world since light was created before the sun. He offers no maudlin consolation; to him the sins of the intellect are worse than the sins of the flesh. He believed in hell, which he never defined, as devoutly as Dante, who did describe it. They both knew their hearts and the world; and the world has never invented any remedy so effective as that which À Kempis offers.

It is the divine remedy of love; but love cannot exist without the fear of hurting or offending the Beloved.

The best book yet written on the causes that made for the World War and on their remedy is "The Rebuilding of Europe," by David Jayne Hill. There we find this quotation from Villari illuminated:

but it would be more exact to say that Machiavelli's work written in 1513 and published in 1532 was the perfect expression of an emancipation from moral restraints far advanced. The Christ-idealism of the Middle Ages had already largely disappeared. The old grounds of obligation had been swept away. Men looked for their safety to the nation-state rather than to the solidarity of Christendom; and the state, as Machiavelli's gospel proclaimed it, consisted in absolute and irresponsible control exercised by one man who should embody its unity, strength, and authority.

Montaigne felt rather than understood the cruelty and brutality of the state traditions of his time; and these traditions were seriously combatted when the United States made brave efforts both at Versailles and Washington. Doctor Hill sums up the essential principles which guided the world from the Renascence to the year 1918:

(1) The essence of a State is "sovereignty," defined as "supreme power." (2) A sovereign State has the right to declare war upon any other sovereign State for any reason that seems to it sufficient. (3) An act of conquest by the exercise of superior military force entitles the conqueror to the possession of the conquered territory. (4) The population goes with the land and becomes subject to the will of the conqueror.

What member of the memorable conference, which began at Washington on November 12, 1921, would have dared to assert these unmoral principles, accepted alike by the Congress of Vienna and the Congress of Berlin, in principle? King John of England looked on their negation as an unholy novelty, though that negation was the leaven of the best of the life of the Middle Ages.

There can be no doubt that the germ of the idea of freedom was kept alive, in the miasma which poisoned "The Prince" and Machiavelli's world, by men like Sir Thomas Browne and Montaigne. A better understanding of the principles of these men would have made Milton less autocratic—Lucifer, though a rebel, was not a democrat—and Voltaire less destructive. And yet

Voltaire, for whom the French Republic lately named a war vessel, was the friend of Frederick the Great and of Catherine II. Doctor Hill, to whom some of the passages in Sir Thomas Browne and Montaigne sent me, says:

Down to the invasion of Belgium in 1914 the most odious crime ever committed against a civilized people was, no doubt, the first partition of Poland; yet at the time not a voice was raised against it. Louis XV. was "infinitely displeased," but he did not even reply to the King of Poland's appeal for help. George III. coolly answered that "justice ought to be the invariable rule of sovereigns"; but concluded, "I fear, however, misfortunes have reached the point where redress can be had from the hands of the Almighty alone." Catherine II. thought justice satisfied when "everyone takes something." Frederick II. wrote to his brother, "The partition will unite the three religions, Greek, Catholic, and Calvinist; for we would take our communion from the same consecrated body, which is Poland." Only Maria Theresa felt a twinge of conscience. She took but she felt the shame of it. She wrote: "We have by our moderation and fidelity to our engagements acquired the confidence, I may venture to say the admiration, of Europe.... One year has lost it all. I confess, it is difficult to endure it, and that nothing in the world has cost me more than the loss of our good name." It is a strange phenomenon that in matters where the unsophisticated human conscience so promptly pronounces judgment and spontaneously condemns, the solid mass of moral conviction should count for nothing in affairs of state. Against it a purely national prejudice has never failed to prevail.

Montaigne does not formulate his comparisons so clearly; nor does Sir Thomas Browne touch so unerringly the canker in the root of the politics of his time; but one cannot saturate oneself in the works of either without contrasting them with the physiocrats of the eighteenth century, who tore up the cockles and the wheat together.

Of all American writers Mr. H. L. Mencken is the most adventurous, and one might almost say the cleverest. He could not be dull if he tried. This is admirably exemplified in "The American Language," which appears in a second edition, revised and enlarged and dated 1921. We are told that Mencken was born in Baltimore on September 12, 1880; that his family has been settled in Maryland for nearly a hundred years; and that he is of mixed ancestry, chiefly German, Irish, and English. He is, therefore, a typical American, and well qualified to write on "The American Language." Mr. Mencken truly says that the weakest courses in our universities are those which concern themselves with written and spoken English. He adds that such grammar as is taught in our schools and colleges

is a grammar standing four-legged upon the theorizings and false inferences of English Latinists of a past generation, eager only to break the wild tongue of Shakespeare to a rule; and its frank aim is to create in us a high respect for a book language which few of us ever actually speak and not many of us even learn to write. That language, elaborately artificial though it may be, undoubtedly has merits. It shows a sonority and a stateliness that you must go to the Latin and the Golden Age to match; its "highly charged and heavy-shotted" periods, in Matthew Arnold's phrase, serve admirably the obscurantist purposes of American pedagogy and of English parliamentary oratory and leader-writing; it is something new for the literary artists of both countries to prove their skill upon by flouting it. But to the average American, bent upon expressing his ideas, not stupendously but merely clearly, it must always remain something vague and remote, like Greek history or the properties of the parabola, for he never speaks it or hears it spoken, and seldom encounters it in his everyday reading. If he learns to write it, which is not often, it is with a rather depressing sense of its artificiality. He may master it as a Korean, bred in the colloquial Onmun, may master the literary Korean-Chinese, but he never thinks in it or quite feels it.

Mr. Mencken is both instructive and destructive; but he is not so constructive as to build a road through the marsh of confusion into which that conflict of dialects in the English language—a language which is grammarless and dependent upon usage—has left us. He tells us that good writing consists, as in the case of Howells, in deliberately throwing overboard the principles so elaborately inculcated, or, as in the case of Lincoln, in standing unaware of them. Whether this is true in the case of Howells or not, it must be remembered that Lincoln was fed, through his reading, on the results of those linguistic principles which are with us in English tradition. It is the usage of Cardinal Newman or Hawthorne or Stevenson or Agnes Repplier, or of Lincoln himself, which those who want to write good English follow rather than the elaborate rules of confused English grammar which are forgotten almost as soon as they are learned.

Personally, in youthful days, I could make nothing out of the "grammar" of the English language until I had begun to study Latin prosody; and then it became clear to me that only a few bones in the structure of English, taken from the Latin practice, were valuable; that the flesh of the English tongue would not fit the whole skeleton.

As the English language, spoken everywhere, must depend on good usage, and the bad usage of to-day often becomes the good usage of to-morrow, it is regrettable that no scientific study of the American vocabulary or of the influences lying at the root of American word-formation—to quote Mr. Mencken—has as yet been made. The elder student was content with correcting the examples of bad English in Blair's "Rhetoric." Later, he read "The Dean's English," very popular at one time, Richard Grant White's

"Words and Their Uses," and perhaps a little book called "The Verbalist." To this, one of the most bewildering books on the manner of writing English ever written, Herbert Spencer's "Philosophy of Style" was added. Whether it is Herbert Spencer's lack of a sense of humour or the fallibility of his theories that has put him somewhat out of date is not easy to say. In no book of his is a sense of humour so lacking as in the "Philosophy of Style." Its principles have a perennial value and nearly every author on style, since Spencer wrote, has repeated them with variations; but Spencer's method of presenting them is as involved as any method adopted by a philosopher could be—and that is saying a good deal.

The English of the universities hold that Americans are the slave of Webster's Dictionary; and this is true of a certain limited class of Americans. The English public speaker allows himself more freedom in the matter of pronunciation than very scrupulous Americans do. Lord Balfour's speeches at the Washington Conference offered several examples of this.

"The Supreme Court of the United States has decided that Webster's Dictionary is *the* American dictionary, and I propose to consider all its decisions as final," said, in hot argument, a New York lawyer who habitually uses "dontcha know" and "I wanta." Shakespeare, he regards as an author whose English ought to be corrected; and he became furious over what he called the mispronunciation of "apotheosis," which he said a favourite preacher had not uttered according to Webster. And I have known literary societies in the South to be disrupted over the use of the word "nasty" by a Northern woman; and, as for "bloody," Mr. Mencken shows us that one of the outrages committed by Mr. Shaw against English convention was his permitting the heroine of "Pygmalion" to use it on the stage. There is one Americanism, however, against which, as far as I can find, Mr. Mencken does not protest. It is the use of the word "consummated" in a phrase like "the marriage was consummated in the First Baptist Church at high noon"!

In spite of democratic disapproval, some will still hold that "lift" is better than "elevator," and "station" better than "dépot." Though these are departures from the current vernacular. We speak English often when our critical friends in England imagine that we are speaking American. I have known a gentleman in New Jersey who has cultivated English traditions of speech, to shrink in horror at the mention of "flap-jack" and "ice-cream." He could never find a substitute in *real* English for "flap-jack," but he always substituted "ices" for "ice-cream." On one occasion I heard him inveigh against the horror of the word "pies," for those "detestable messy things sold by the ton to the uncivilized"; and he spent the time of lunch in pointing out that no such composition really existed in polite society; but when his "cook general" was seen approaching with an unmistakable "pie," the kind supposed by the readers of advertisements to be made by "mothers," and ordered hastily because of the coming of the unexpected guest, he was cast down. The guest tried to save the situation by speaking of the obnoxious pastry as "a tart." The host shook his head—"a tart," in English, could never be covered!

Mr. Mencken shows us that "flap-jack," "molasses," "home-spun," "ice-cream" are old English; that "Bub," which used to shock London visitors to Old Philadelphia, is a bit of provincial English; and that "muss" is found in "Antony and Cleopatra." I wish I had known that when I was young; it would have saved me a bad mark for paraphrasing "Menelaus and Paris got into a muss over Helen." But probably the use of "row" to express that little difficulty would not have saved me!

The best judge of Madeira in Philadelphia always said "cheer" for "chair" and "sasser" for "saucer" and "tay" for "tea" and "obleged" for "obliged"; and he drank from his saucer, too; and his table was always provided with little dishes, like butter plates, for the discarded cups. His example gave me a profound contempt for those newly rich in learning who laugh without understanding, who are the slaves of the dictionary, and who are so "vastly" meticulous. This old gentleman was an education in himself; he had lived at the "English court"—or near it—and when he came to visit us once a year, we listened enraptured. I once fell from grace; but not from my reverence for him, by making a mistake in my search for knowledge which involved his age. It was very easy to ask him whether Anne Boleyn had asked for a "cheer" but not easy to escape from the family denunciation that followed. It seemed that he had not lived at or near the court of Henry VIII!

Mr. Mencken explains why the use of "sick" for "ill" is taboo in England, except among the very youngest Realists. And, by the way, Mr. Hugh Walpole in "The Young Enchanted" goes so far in one of the speeches of the atrocious Mrs. Tennsen, that the shocking word "bloody" used by Mr. Bernard Shaw on one famous occasion sinks into a pastel tint! Mr. Mencken says:

The Pilgrims brought over with them the English of James I. and the Authorized Version, and their descendants of a century later, inheriting it, allowed the fundamentals to be but little changed by the academic overhauling that the mother tongue was put to during the early part of the Eighteenth Century.

The Bible won against the prudery of the new English; prudery will go very far, and I can recall the objection of an evangelical lady, in Philadelphia, who disliked the nightly saying of the "Ave Maria" by a little Papist relative. This was not on religious grounds; it was because of "blessed is the fruit of thy womb, Jesus," in the prayer. The little Papist had been taught to repeat the salutation of the Angel Gabriel in Latin, so, at bedtime, he changed to

"Benedictus fructus ventris tui" and the careful lady thought it sounded "more decent"!

Poker players may be interested in Mr. Mencken's revelation that "ante" came into our language through the Spanish; he says,

cinch was borrowed from the Spanish "cincha" in the early Texas days, though its figurative use did not come in until much later.

It is pleasant to note the soundness of Mr. Mencken's judgment in regard to that very great philologer, the Dane, Doctor Jespersen, and he quotes, in favour of the clarity and directness of the English language, another great Dane, Doctor Thomson. Doctor Jespersen admits that our tongue has a certain masculine ungainliness. It has rare elements of strength in its simplicity. In English the subject almost invariably precedes the verb and the object follows it; even in English poetry this usage is seldom violated. In Tennyson, its observance might be counted at 80,

but in the poetry of Holger Drachmann, the Dane, it falls to 61, in Anatole France's prose, to 66, in Gabriele d' Annunzio to 49, and in the poetry of Goethe to 30.

That our language has only five vowels, which have to do duty for more than a score of sounds, is a grave fault; and the unhappy French preacher who, from an English pulpit, pronounced "plough" as "pluff" had much excuse. But on the other hand, why do the French make us say "fluer de lis," instead of "fleur de lee"? And "Rheims"? How many conversational pitfalls is "Rheims" responsible for!

There is no book that ought to give the judicious such quiet pleasure or more food for thought or for stimulating conversation than Mr. Mencken's "The American Language," except Burton's "Anatomy of Melancholy," Boswell's "Johnson," the "Devout Life" of Saint Francis de Sales, Pepys's "Diary," the "Letters" of Madame de Sévigné, Beveridge's "Life" of Marshall, and the "Memoirs" of Gouverneur Morris! It is a book for odd moments; yet it is a temptation to continuous reading; and a precious treasure is its bibliography! And how pleasant it is to verify the quotations in a library; preferably with the snow falling in thick flakes, and an English victim who cannot escape, even after dinner is announced. Mr. Mencken is a benefactor!

It is very remarkable that Mr. Mencken's audacious disregard of English grammar in theory has not impaired the clearness of his point of view and of his own style. If dead authors could write after the manner in which Mr. Andrew Lang has written to them, I should like to read Herbert Spencer's opinions of Mr. Mencken's volumes. If Sir Oliver Lodge and Sir Conan Doyle want really to please a small but discriminating public, let them induce Herbert Spencer to analyze Mr. Mencken's statements on the growth of the

English language! In my time we were expected to take Spencer's "Philosophy of Style" very seriously. There is no doubt that his principles have been repeated by every writer on style, including Dr. Barrett Wendell in his important "English Composition," since Mr. Spencer wrote; but the method of Spencer's expression of his principles reminds one of the tangled wood in which Dante languished before he met Beatrice.

There is no doubt that Mr. Spencer makes us think of writing as a science and art; his philosophy of style is right enough. But while he provokes puzzled thought, he does no more. There is more meat in Robert Louis Stevenson's "A College Magazine" than in all the complications in style in the brochure of the idol of the eighties.

And a greater stylist than even Stevenson is the author of a little volume which I keep by my side ever since Mr. Frederick O'Brien and the terrifying Gaugain have turned us to the islands of the Pacific. It is Charles Warren Stoddard's "South Sea Idyls." And if one wants to know how to read for pleasure or comfort—for reading or writing does not come by nature—there is "Moby Dick," by Herman Melville, the close friend of the Hawthornes and a writer so American that Mr. Mencken must love him. But he ought to be read as a novelist.

Mr. Herbert Spencer and "The South Sea Idyls" bring the *flâneur*—the chief business of a *flâneur* of the pavements (we were forbidden in old Philadelphia to say "sidewalks") is to look into unrelated shop-windows; but the *flâneur* among books finds none of his shop-windows unrelated—back to Mr. Mencken, who does not give us the genesis of a word that sounded something like "sadie." It meant "thank you." Every Pennsylvania child used it, until the elegants interfered, and they often did interfere. You might say "apothecary" or "chemist"; but you should never say "druggist." I trust that it is no breach of confidence to repeat that the devout and very distinguished of modern Philadelphians, Mr. John Drew, discovered that there were two languages in his neighbourhood, one for the ears of his parents and one for the boys in the street. One was very much in the position of the Yorkshire lad I met the other day. "But you haven't a Yorkshire accent!" "No, sir," he said, "my parents whipped it out of me." But there is, in New York City, at least the beginning of one American language—the language of the street.

In considering the impression that books have usually made on me, I have often asked myself why they are such an unfailing source of pleasure and even of joy. Every reader has, of course, his own answer to this. For the plots of novels, I have always had very little respect, although I believe, with Anthony Trollope, that a plot is absolutely necessary to a really good novel, and that it is the very soul of a romance. Of memoirs—even the apocryphal writings of the Marquise de Créquy have always been very agreeable to me; I have never been so dull or so tired, that I could not find some solace in the Diary of Mr. Pepys, in the Autobiography of Franklin, in the peerless journal of Mr. Boswell; and even the revelations of Madame Campan, as a last resource, were worth returning to. As for the diary of Madame d'Arblay, it reproduces so admirably the struggles of a bright spirit against the dullest of all atmospheres, that it seems like a new discovery in psychology. And now comes Professor Tinker's "Young Boswell" and those precious diaries including that of Mrs. Pepys by a certain E. Barrington. Life *is* worth living!

I must confess that I have never found any poet excepting King David whom I liked because he taught me anything. Didactic "poetry" wearies me, probably because it is not poetry at all. When people praise Thompson's "Hound of Heaven," because it is dogmatic, I am surprised—for if I found anything dogmatic in it, it would lose all its splendour for me. The Apocalypse and "The Hound of Heaven" are glorious visions of truth at a white heat.

Tennyson's "Two Voices" loses all its value when it ceases to be a picture and becomes an important sermon. And as for Spenser, the didactic symbolism of his "Faerie Queen" might be lost forever with no great disadvantage to posterity if his splendid "Epithalamion" could be preserved. Browning's optimism has always left me cold, and I never could quite understand why most of his readers have set him down as a great philosopher. All may be well with the world, but I could never see that Browning's poetry proved it in any way. When the time comes for a cultivated English world—a thoughtful English-speaking world—to weigh the merits of English-speaking poets, Browning will be found among the first. Who has done anything finer in English than "A Grammarian's Funeral"? Or "My Last Duchess," or "A Toccata of Galuppi's" or some of the passages in "Pippa Passes"? Who has conceived a better fable for a poem than that of "Pippa"? And as for Keats, the world he discovered for us is of greater value to the faculties of the mind than all the philosophies of Wordsworth.

To me, the intense delight I have in novels and poems is due to their power of taking me out of myself, of enlightening me as to my own faults and peculiarities, not by preaching but by example, and of raising me to a higher plane of toleration and of gaiety of heart.

As I grow older, I find that the phrase Stevenson once applied to works of fiction becomes more and more regrettable. He compared the followers of this consoling art to "*filles de joie.*" He doubtless meant that these goddesses— "*les filles de joie*" are always young—gave us visions of the joy of life; that they might be sensuous without being sensual; but his phrase falls far short of the truth. There are novels, like Mrs. Jackson's "Ramona," which are joyous and serious at once. Or take "The Cardinal's Snuff Box" or "Pepita Jiminez."

Every constant reader has his favourite essayists. As a rule, he reads them to be soothed or to be amused. In making my confession, I must say that only a few of the essayists really amuse me. They are, as a rule, more witty than humorous, and generally they make one self-conscious, being self-conscious themselves. There are a hundred different types of the essayist. Each of us has his favourite bore among them. Once I found all the prose works of a fine poet and friend of mine, Aubrey de Vere, on the shelves of a constant reader. "Why?" I asked. "The result of a severe sense of duty!" he said.

Madame Roland tried hard for a title of nobility and failed, though she gained in the end a greater title. Her works are insufferably and complacently conceited, and yet I always look at their bindings with respect. Mrs. Blashfield, who died too soon, has given us, in her first volume—unfortunately the only one—a new view of this Empress of Didacticism. It is strange indeed that Madame Roland could have been nourished by that most stimulating of all books—"The Devout Life of St. Francis de Sales." Monseigneur de Sales is, to my mind, the most practical of all the essayists, even when he puts his essays in the form of letters. Next comes Fénelon's and—I know that I shall shock those who regard his philosophy as merely Deistic—next comes, for his power of stimulation, Emerson.

It has certainly occurred to me, perhaps too late, that these confessions may be taken as didactic in themselves; in writing them I have had not the slightest intention of improving anybody's mind but simply of relieving my own, by button-holing the reader who happens to come my way. I should like to add that what is called the coarseness of the eighteenth-century novel and romance is much more healthful than the nasty brutality of a school of our novelists—who make up for their lack of talent and of wide experience by trying to excite animal instincts. Eroticism may be delicately treated; but art has nothing in common with the process of "cooking stale cabbage over farthing candles," to use Charles Reade's phrase.

If my habit of constant reading had not taught me the value of calmness and patience, I should like to say, with violent emphasis, that a reason for thanking God is that Americans have produced a literature—the continuation of an older literature with variations, it is true,—that has added to the glory of civilization. To prove this, I need mention only one book, "The Scarlet Letter," and I am glad to end my book by writing the name of Hawthorne. Literary comparisons with England, or with France, Italy, Spain, or any of the other continental nations, are no longer to our disadvantage. It is the fashion of the American who writes of American books to put—in his own mind, at least—a title to his discourse that reminds me of Miss Blanche

Amory's "Mes Larmes." It is an outworn tradition. American literature is robust enough for smiles.

It can smile and laugh. It can be serious and not self-conscious. It is rapidly taking to itself all the best traditions of the older literature and assimilating them. Christopher Morley and Heywood Broun and Don Marquis and Mencken write—at their best—as lightly and as trippingly as any past master of the *feuilleton*. There is nobody writing in the daily press in Paris to-day who does the *feuilleton* as well as they do it. If you ask me whether I, as a constant reader, pay much attention to what they say, I shall answer, No. But their method is the thing. Will they live? Of course not. Is Émile de Girardin alive? Or all the clever ones that James Huneker found buried and could not revive? One still reads the "Portraits de Femmes," of Sainte-Beuve; but Sainte-Beuve was something more than a "columnist." And these folk will be, too, in time! At any rate, they are good enough for the present.

Who, writing in French or in any language, *outre-mer*, does better, or as well, as Holliday? And where is the peer of Charles S. Brooks in "Hints to Pilgrims"? "Luca Sarto," the best novel of old Italian life by an American—since Mrs. Wharton's "Valley of Decision"—proved him to be a fine artist. He perhaps knew his period better psychologically than Mrs. Wharton, but here there's room for argument. Mrs. Wharton, although she is an admirable artist, grows indifferent and insular at long intervals.

"Luca Sarto" dropped like the gentle rain from heaven; and then came "Hints to Pilgrims." This I wanted to write about in the *Yale Review*, but the selfish editor, Mr. Cross, said that he preferred to keep it for himself!

"Hints to Pilgrims" is the essence of the modern essay. Strangely enough, it sent me back to the "Colour of Life" by the only real *précieuse* living in our world to-day, Alice Meynell; and I read that with new delight between certain paragraphs in Brooks's paper "On Finding a Plot." Why is not "Hints to Pilgrims" in its fourteenth edition? Or why has it no *claque*? The kind of *claque* that is so common now—which opens suddenly like a chorus of cicadas in the "Idylls of Theocritus"? After all, your education must have been well begun before you can enjoy "Hints to Pilgrims," while for "Huckleberry Finn" the less education you have, the better. Mr. Brooks writes:

Let us suppose, for example, that Carmen, before she got into that ugly affair with the Toreador, had settled down in Barchester beneath the towers. Would the shadow of the cloister, do you think, have cooled her Southern blood? Would she have conformed to the decent gossip of the town? Or, on the contrary, does not a hot colour always tint the colder mixture? Suppose that Carmen came to live just outside the Cathedral close and walked every morning with her gay parasol and her pretty swishing skirts past the Bishop's window.

We can fancy his pen hanging dully above his sermon, with his eyes on space for any wandering thought, as if the clouds, like treasure ships upon a sea, were freighted with riches for his use. The Bishop is brooding on an address to the Ladies' Sewing Guild. He must find a text for his instructive finger. It is a warm spring morning and the daffodils are waving in the borders of the grass. A robin sings in the hedge with an answer from his mate. There is wind in the tree-tops with lively invitation to adventure, but the Bishop is bent to his sober task. Carmen picks her way demurely across the puddles in the direction of the Vicarage. Her eyes turn modestly toward his window. Surely she does not see him at his desk. That dainty inch of scarlet stocking is quite by accident. It is the puddles and the wind frisking with her skirt.

"Eh! Dear me!" The good man is merely human. He pushes up his spectacles for nearer sight. He draws aside the curtain. "Dear me! Bless my soul! Who is the lady? Quite a foreign air. I don't remember her at our little gatherings for the heathen." A text is forgotten. The clouds are empty caravels. He calls to Betsy, the housemaid, for a fresh neckcloth and his gaiters. He has recalled a meeting with the Vicar and goes out whistling softly, to disaster.

You do not find delightful fooling like this every day; and there is much more of it. Take this:

Suppose, for a better example, that the cheerful Mark Tapley, who always came out strong in adversity, were placed in a modern Russian novel. As the undaunted Taplovitch he would have shifted its gloom to a sunny ending. Fancy our own dear Pollyanna, the glad girl, adopted by an aunt in "Crime and Punishment." Even Dostoyevsky must have laid down his doleful pen to give her at last a happy wedding—flower-girls and angel-food, even a shrill soprano behind the hired palms and a table of cut glass.

Oliver Twist and Nancy—merely acquaintances in the original story—with a fresh hand at the plot, might have gone on a bank holiday to Margate. And been blown off shore. Suppose that the whole excursion was wrecked on Treasure Island and that everyone was drowned except Nancy, Oliver, and perhaps the trombone player of the ships' band, who had blown himself so full of wind for fox-trots on the upper deck that he couldn't sink. It is Robinson Crusoe, lodging as a handsome bachelor on the lonely island—observe the cunning of the plot!—who battles with the waves and rescues Nancy. The movie-rights alone of this are worth a fortune. And then Crusoe, Oliver, Friday, and the trombone player stand a siege from John Silver and Bill Sikes, who are pirates, with Spanish doubloons in a hidden cove. And Crusoe falls in love with Nancy. Here is a tense triangle. But youth goes to youth. Crusoe's whiskers are only dyed their glossy black. The trombone player, by good luck (you see now why he was saved from the wreck), is discovered to be a retired clergyman—doubtless a Methodist. The happy knot is tied. And then—a sail! A sail! Oliver and Nancy settle down in a semi-detached near London, with oyster shells along the garden path and cat-tails in the umbrella jar. The story ends prettily under their plane-tree at the rear—tea for three, with a trombone solo, and the faithful Friday and Old Bill, reformed now, as gardener, clipping together the shrubs against the sunny wall.

When I found Brooks, I felt again the pang of loss, that Theodore Roosevelt had not read "Hints to Pilgrims," before he passed into "the other room" and eternal light shone upon him! He would have discovered "Hints to Pilgrims," and celebrated it as soon as any of us.

How he loved books! And he seemed to have read all the right things in his youth; you forgot time and kicked Black Care away when he talked with you about them. He could drop from Dante to Brillat-Savarin (in whom he had not much interest, since he was a *gourmet* and did not regard sausages as the highest form of German art!) and his descents and ascents from book to book were as smooth as Melba's sliding scales—and her scales were smoother than Patti's.

Do you remember his "Dante in the Bowery," and "The Ancient Irish Sagas"? He caught fire at the quotation from the "Lament of Deirdre"; and concluded at once that the Celts were the only people who, before Christianity invented chivalry, understood the meaning of romantic love. It is a great temptation to write at length on the books he liked, and how he fought for them, and explained them, and lived with them. Thinking of him, the most constant of book-lovers, I can only say, "Farewell and Hail!"

[2] Mr. Walpole has almost forfeited the allegiance of people who admired his quality of well-bred distinction by writing in "The Young Enchanted" of George Eliot as a "horse-faced genius."

THE END

CPSIA information can be obtained
at www.ICGtesting.com
Printed in the USA
LVHW031247310522
720087LV00005B/687